We All Believed Indian

The Life and Prosperity of a Mixed Blood Tribal
Elder on the Flathead Indian Reservation,
Montana,

1897-1995

by
Charles McDonald

Charles Duncan McDonald

We All Believed Indian

The Life and Prosperity of a Mixed Blood Tribal
Elder on the Flathead Indian Reservation,
Montana,

1897-1995

by
Charles McDonald

edited by
Robert Bigart and Joseph McDonald

interviews by
Laurie Mercier, Thompson Smith, and Roy Bigcrane

published by
Salish Kootenai College Press
Pablo, Montana

distributed by
University of Nebraska Press
Lincoln, Nebraska

2018

Cover design: Corwin "Corky" Clairmont, artist/graphic designer, Pablo, Montana
Cover illustration and frontpiece: Charles Duncan McDonald, courtesy Confederated Salish and Kootenai Tribes, Pablo, Montana.

Library of Congress Cataloging-in-Publication Data:
Names: McDonald, Charles, 1897-1995, author. | Bigart, Robert, editor. |
    McDonald, Joseph, 1933- editor.
Title: We all believed Indian : the life and prosperity of a mixed blood tribal
    elder on the Flathead Indian Reservation, Montana, 1897-1995 / by Charles
    McDonald ; edited by Robert Bigart and Joseph McDonald ; interviews by
    Laurie Mercier, Thompson Smith, and Roy Bigcrane.
Description: Pablo, Montana : Salish Kootenai College Press, 2018.
Identifiers: LCCN 2018028861 | ISBN 9781934594216 (pbk.)
Subjects: LCSH: Salish Indians--Montana--Biography. | Kootenai Indians-
    -Montana--Biography. | Indian leadership--Montana--Flathead Indian
    Reservation--History--20th century. | Salish Indians--Montana--
    Government relations. | Kootenai Indians--Montana--Government relations.
    | Confederated Salish & Kootenai Tribes of the Flathead Reservation,
    Montana--History--20th century. | Flathead Indian Reservation (Mont.)-
    -History--20th century. | McDonald, Charles, 1897-1995. | LCGFT:
    Autobiographies.
Classification: LCC E99.S2 M34 2018 | DDC 978.6004/979435--dc23
LC record available at https://lccn.loc.gov/2018028861

Distributed by University of Nebraska Press, 1111 Lincoln Mall, Lincoln, NE
68588-0630, order 1-800-755-1105, www.nebraskapress.unl.edu.

Table of Contents

Historical Preface

The Salish and Kootenai Indian tribes of the Flathead Reservation in western Montana have a long and storied history. They lived for centuries in the Northern Rocky Mountains and Northeastern Great Plains on the abundance of natural resources the land provided.

In the eighteenth century they acquired horses and expanded their hunting range in the Great Plains. The Salish and Kootenai were rich in horses compared to the Plains tribes, but the Plains tribes had better access to guns at the northern trading posts. The Plains tribes, especially the Blackfeet, were larger, wanted Salish and Kootenai horses, and had superior fire power. By the start of the nineteenth century, when the Lewis and Clark Expedition entered western Montana, the Salish and Kootenai were anxious to ally with the white men and other Rocky Mountain tribes against the Blackfeet war parties. The Salish and Kootenai accepted Christian missionaries to secure help from the white men's supernatural powers.

In the nineteenth century, the alliance with the whites continued even through the 1855 Hellgate Treaty and the explosion of the white population in the second half of the century. By the end of the nineteenth century, the decimation of the buffalo and other wild game and plant resources forced the tribes to develop new ways to make a living. Cattle and horse raising and farming became the base of the Flathead Reservation economy. Traditional hunting and gathering continued, but they could now only supplement livestock and farming. By 1900, the tribes had made the painful economic adjustments and were still self-supporting.

At the start of the twentieth century, the tribes were faced with new and serious assaults on the reservation from the allotment policy. This federal policy was imposed on the tribes without their consent by Joseph Dixon, a white Montana politician. The policy involved assigning individual land allotments to all tribal members and then selling the "surplus" land to white homesteaders at bargain prices. This theft of tribal resources left many tribal members impoverished.

Allotment and white homesteading was the context for the life story and experiences of Charles Duncan McDonald told in this book. Charlie witnessed and was part of the long struggle of the Confederated Salish and Kootenai Tribes to come back from the devastating theft of tribal assets and power. The allotment and irrigation program of the twentieth century caused much financial damage and ecological change on the reservation. Charlie tells how the tribal community fought back to ensure the political and economic survival of the tribes. When he died in 1995, the Confederated Salish and Kootenai Tribes were much more secure and influential than they had been in 1897, when he was born. Charlie's story of prosperity and survival shows how the efforts of individual tribal members were able to build a future for new generations of tribal members.

Charles Duncan McDonald:
An Appreciation

It is fun to write about my Uncle Charlie. I remember him as a kind and loving person. He was always glad to see you and wanted to know what a person was doing. He was always pleased and proud of any accomplishments his friends and family made. The first thing he would ask when you came into his house was, "Did you eat?" or "Have you et?" His cute little wife Achsah would get up and start preparing something, and it always tasted good.

Charlie always dressed in a long sleeve wool shirt, gabardine trousers, and high-top boots with laces. He wore rimless glasses and always had a pen in his shirt pocket. In later years he wore a hearing aid and would adjust it while visiting. When he left the house, he wore a broad brimmed western style hat. I never knew him to wear overalls or waist high denim pants like Levis or Wranglers that have been popular for the past several years.

He was an exceptionally good story teller. He spoke slowly and clearly and was quite accurate in his recollection of past events in his life. He was especially good at names of people and each person's family ancestry. Charlie could recall tribal gatherings, war dances (he didn't like the name "powwow"), agency meetings, government policy changes and rulings, natural disasters such as forest fires, and how people lived during the changing times of the 1900s.

He lived through and could recall particular events of the pre-allotment period, the allotment period, the homesteading period, the irrigation construction, World War I, the depression, World War II, and the post war years into the 1990s. He could relate the social impact and the change in lifestyles as the Indian people adjusted to the always changing times. He could recall certain individual

Indians and families, and the struggles they had to survive through this tumultuous period of time.

Charlie's life story is a great example of a mixed blood with strong Indian affiliations living through the 1900s. He always claimed to think and be Indian, even though he was half white. He became an important link between the federal government and the Indian people of the reservation. He was often called upon by Bureau of Indian Affairs officials to be their interpreter when doing business with non-English speaking Indian people.

He was never one to talk disparaging about white people. He interacted with them easily and was one to see both sides of an issue and have compassion for everyone.

In the following book, he tells much of his life story and provides insight into the way of life of the local people in the early 1900s and through the middle and later years of the century. We are all grateful for Charlie's generosity in sharing his stories and personal views of events that impacted the social structure and environment of the Flathead Indian Reservation during the 1900s.

Joe McDonald

Editors' Introduction

Welcome to Charlie McDonald's book.

Charles Duncan McDonald was a widely respected elder of the Confederated Salish and Kootenai Tribes of the Flathead Indian Reservation. During his long life between 1897 and 1995, he was eyewitness to almost a century of economic and political change on the reservation. He experienced the loss of his allotment and the hard times of the depression years in the late 1910s, the 1920s, and the 1930s.

Charlie relays memories and family lore about the McDonald's on the Flathead Reservation. Over the years, the McDonalds have provided many important political and economic leaders for the tribes.

He could remember many of the most dramatic events affecting the Flathead Reservation tribes in the twentieth century. The 1908 killing of tribal members and a Montana state game warden in the Swan Valley, was just the most dramatic event in the tribes' century long battle to protect their treaty-guaranteed hunting rights. The 1908-1909 round up of the Pablo buffalo herd for shipment to Canada was part of the end of open range grazing that resulted from opening the reservation to white homesteaders. Charlie, and some of his relatives, were also eyewitnesses to the construction of the Flathead Lake dam. The valuable dam site at the foot of the lake was a prize fought over by white speculators, large corporations, and government regulatory agencies between the passage of the Flathead allotment bill in 1904 and the early 1930s, when construction began in earnest.

While these dramatic events were swirling around the tribes, Charlie was cowboying around reservation ranches and packing for the United States Forest Service. He worked for the U.S. Forest Service as a packer around western Montana as the Forest Service expanded its fire control efforts in the early 1930s.

Charlie played a personal role in tribal history as a member of the first tribal council, organized under the Wheeler-Howard Act in 1935. He, and the other early councilmen, struggled to get the tribes' voice heard in reservation affairs. As a councilman, and later as a tribal employee, he witnesses the slow growth of the economic and political power of the Confederated Salish and Kootenai Tribes between 1935 and the end of the twentieth century.

He witnessed the ecological changes brought on the reservation by the introduction of irrigation and the expanding population of white homesteaders. His memories of these changes add important context to the political events that buffeted the reservation during the period.

Charlie was either an eyewitness or heard firsthand accounts of most of the tumultuous events on the Flathead Reservation during the twentieth century. In his later years, his excellent memory and willingness to share his experiences made him a frequent source of reservation history.

There is some confusion about Charlie's proper name. He was listed as Duncan Charles McDonald in the Flathead Agency records, but as Charles Duncan McDonald in his baptism record at the St. Ignatius Mission. According to the church records he was born on November 17, 1897, and baptized on January 5, 1898. The editors have used Charles Duncan McDonald to help distinguish Charlie from his uncle, Duncan McDonald.

In this book the editors have amalgamated transcripts of some of Charlie's oral history interviews into a single manuscript about his life and reservation history during the twentieth century. Most of the book is chronological, which required us to rearrange the order of some portions of the interview transcripts. When Charlie discussed the same events in different interviews, we used the most detailed description for the book. The topics covered in the book were determined by the interests and questions of the different interviewers. We have tried to only lightly edit the material. Some words have been inserted in brackets where we felt they made his meaning easier to follow. We have not corrected his grammar, but we have deleted the "hems" and "ahs" of spoken communication. Hopefully we have ended up with a readable manuscript which is still in Charlie's voice.

The manuscript is a synthesis of several different oral history interviews during Charlie's later years:

1. Laurie Mercier interviewed Charlie on April 20 and 23, 1982, for the Montanans at Work Project, an oral history project conducted by the Montana Historical Society. The tapes of these interviews are now Oral History 262 at the Research Library of the Montana Historical Society in Helena. The material from the Mercier interviews is published with the permission of the Montana Historical Society.

2. Thompson Smith and Roy Bigcrane recorded ten video tapes of interviews with Charlie as part of their research for *The Place of Falling Waters*, a video about the Flathead Lake dam produced at the Media Center, Salish Kootenai College, Pablo, Montana. These interviews were conducted on September 16 and October 6, 1988.

3. Thompson Smith and Roy Bigcrane interviewed Charlie in 1992 at the Big Bend of the Flathead River.

4. Thompson Smith also recorded an interview with Charlie on October 2, 1991, on Finley Creek (Marsh Creek) and Post Creek on the reservation.

Charlie is no longer with us. Hopefully this lightly edited version of his oral history interviews will provide a window for later generations to profit from his memories and wisdom.

Robert Bigart
Joseph McDonald

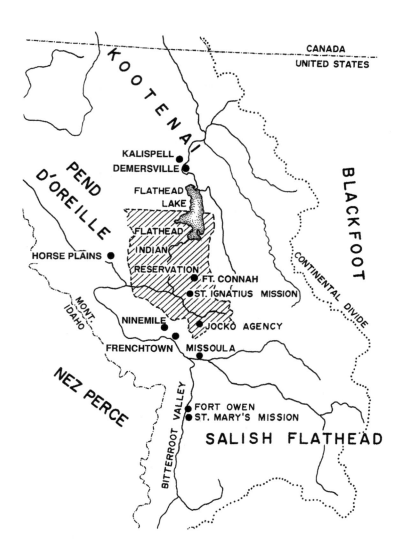

**Flathead Indian Reservation
Showing Tribal Territories
and Surrounding Towns**

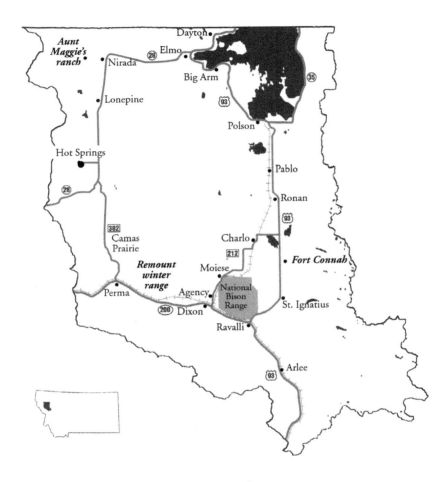

Flathead Indian Reservation, Montana

Map by Wyatt Design, Helena, Montana.

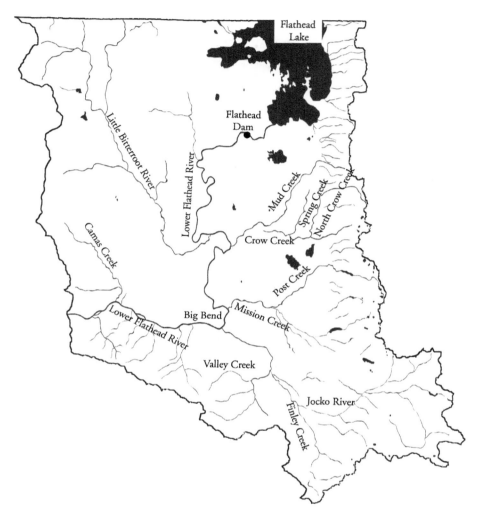

Flathead Indian Reservation, Montana,
Watersheds

Map by Wyatt Design, Helena, Montana.

Charles Duncan McDonald: An Outline of His Life

1897 — born to Joseph A. McDonald and Lucy Deschamps McDonald, Post Creek.

1908 or 1909 — attended Ronan government school.

1910 — reservation opened to white homesteaders.

1912–1913 — attended Chemewa Indian School in Oregon.

1913 — moved to Nirada to his uncle's ranch.

1916–1918 — attended Cushman Indian Trade School, Tacoma, Washington.

1919 — got patent for his allotment.

1921 — married Achsah Berry.

1927 — sacked flour in St. Ignatius mission flour mill.

1928–1934 — seasonal packer and worker for U.S. Forest Service.

1935 — Confederated Salish and Kootenai Tribes tribal constitution approved under Indian Reorganization Act or Wheeler Howard Act.

1936–1940 — member of Confederated Salish and Kootenai Tribal Council.

1938 — oldest daughter, Charlotte Achsah McDonald died in accidental drowning in Lone Pine Reservoir.

1942 — moved to Dixon and worked for Bureau of Indian Affairs.

1944 — moved to St. Ignatius.

1960s–1970s — director of Confederated Salish and Kootenai Tribes commodity program.

1995 — Charlie died at Ronan hospital.

Children of Angus McDonald and Catherine McDonald:

| John | Christine | Duncan | Donald | Annie | Maggie | Tom | Alexander | Archie | Joseph A. + Lucy Deschamps | Angus C. | Mary |

Child of Angus McDonald:

| Angus P. |

Children of Joseph A. and Lucy Deschamps McDonald:

| John | Mary | Florence | Charles Duncan + Achsah Berry | Julie | Benny | Daniel | Edward | Walter | Mary |

Children of Charles Duncan and Achsah Berry McDonald:

| Charlotte Achsah | Alta Jane |

Family Tree of Charles Duncan McDonald

McDonald Family Members Referred to in Manuscript

Altie (daugher) — Alta Jane McDonald, Charlie's second daughter.

Angus — Charlie's cousin in WW I, had MS, son of Angus P. McDonald.

Archie McDonald — Charlie's cousin and mediator on Kerr Dam construction.

aunt Emma — Charlie's aunt on his mother's side, the Deschamps family, Fanny "Emma" Niles.

aunt Maggie McDonald — Charlie's aunt with ranch in Nirada.

Bearhead Swaney — Charlie's nephew who accompanied fishing trip on Flathead River.

Berry, Chas. W. — Charlie's father-in-law, Missoula County sheriff, Rankin relative.

Berry, Ida Gregg — Charlie's mother-in-law.

Boneparte, Alex — Charlie's granduncle, enrolled Nez Perce Indian.

Burland, Dennis — Charlie's grandson who worked for David Harriman.

Christine McDonald — Christina MacDonald MacKenzie Williams, Charlie's paternal aunt.

cousin Tom — Kootenai Tom, son of Angus P. McDonald, Charlie's uncle.

cousin who died in 1905 — Peter Colville McDonald, son of Duncan McDonald, Charlie's dad's older brother.

cousin who lived in Nirada, female — Margaret McDonald, killed with her boyfriend, Jimmy Bowman.

dad — Joseph A. McDonald, born in Marcus, Washington, to Angus and Catherine McDonald.

daughter, eldest — Charlotte Achsah McDonald, drowned, July 9, 1938.

Deschamps, Ed — Charlie's mother's brother.

Deschamps, grandma — Charlie's maternal grandmother, Mary Rodgers Collins Deschamps.

Deschamps, grandpa — Charlie's maternal grandfather, Joseph Deschamps, part Shoshoni, husband of Mary Rodgers; father of Lucy Deschamps McDonald, wife of Joe A. McDonald.

Duncan McDonald — Charlie's dad's older brother.

Ed McDonald — Charlie's brother.

Gird, Joe — Charlie's cousin.

Goode, Maggie McDonald — Charlie's niece or second cousin, had Nirada ranch after Maggie McDonald, Charlie's aunt.

grandmother McDonald — Catherine McDonald, Charlie's paternal grandmother and wife of Angus McDonald, fur trader.

grandson who worked for David Harriman — Dennis Burland.

Joe Franklin McDonald — Charlie's nephew, who accompanied fishing trip on Flathead River.

Joe McDonald — Joseph A. McDonald, Charlie's father.

Kootenai Tom — Charlie's cousin, son of Angus P. McDonald.

Ladderoute, Joe — married Charlie's cousin, Rita McDonald.

Maggie McDonald Goode — Charlie's niece or second cousin, had Nirada ranch after Maggie McDonald, Charlie's aunt.

McDonald, Achsah Berry — Charlie's wife.

McDonald, Alta Jane — Charlie's second daughter.

McDonald, Angus — Charlie's paternal grandfather and Hudson's Bay Company trader.

McDonald, Angus — Charlie's cousin in WW I, had MS, son of Angus P. McDonald.

McDonald, Angus C. — Charlie's uncle at Post Creek, his father's full brother.

McDonald, Angus P. — Charlie's uncle, his father's half-brother, part Okanagan; ran family ranch at Nirada with Charlie's Aunt Maggie McDonald.

McDonald, Archie — Charlie's cousin and mediator on Kerr Dam construction.

McDonald, Catherine — Charlie's paternal grandmother and wife of Angus McDonald, fur trader.

McDonald, Charlotte Achsah — Charlie's eldest daughter, drowned, July 9, 1938.

McDonald, Christine — Christina MacDonald McKenzie Williams, Charlie's paternal aunt.

McDonald, Duncan — Charlie's dad's older brother.

McDonald, Ed — Charlie's brother.

McDonald, Joseph Alexander — Charlie's father.

McDonald, Joseph Franklin — Charlie's nephew, who accompanied fishing trip on Flathead River and is co-editor of this manuscript.

McDonald, Maggie — Charlie's aunt with ranch in Nirada. Maggie McDonald Goode runs the Nirada ranch now.

McDonald, Margaret — Charlie's cousin who lived in Nirada and was killed with her boyfriend, Jimmy Bowman.

McDonald, Peter Colville — son of Duncan McDonald, Charlie's uncle.

McDonald, Tom — Kootenai Tom, Charlie's cousin, son of Angus P. McDonald.

McDonald, Tom — Charlie's uncle, son of Angus McDonald, the HBC fur trader, born on Dearborn River.

McDonald, Walter — Charlie's brother.

mother — Lucy Deschamps McDonald, wife of Joseph A. McDonald.

niece — Maggie McDonald Goode, Charlie's niece or second cousin, had Nirada ranch after Maggie McDonald, Charlie's aunt.

Niles, Fanny "Emma" — Charlie's aunt Emma on his mother's side, the Deschamps family.

Rodgers, great grandpa — William Rodgers, mixed blood fur trader, father of Mary Rodgers Collins Deschamps, Charlie's maternal grandmother.

sister — Florence McDonald Smith.

Smith, Florence McDonald — Charlie's sister.

Swaney, Bearhead — Charlie's nephew who accompanied fishing trip on Flathead River.

uncle at Nirada ranch — Angus P. McDonald, Charlie's dad's half-brother, part Okanagan.

uncle at Post Creek — Angus C. McDonald, Charlie's father's full brother.

uncle Tom — Charlie's uncle, Tom McDonald, son of Angus McDonald, the HBC fur trader, born on Dearborn River.

Walter McDonald — Charlie's brother.

Whiting, Ruth — Charlie's niece.

wife — Achsah L. Berry McDonald.

wife's dad — Chas. W. Berry, Missoula County sheriff, Rankin relative.

wife's mother — Ida Gregg Berry, with Sophie Morigeau.

Williams, Christine MacDonald MacKenzie — Charlie's paternal aunt.

Chapter 1

Family and Younger Years

The McDonald Family

I don't remember my grandfather Angus McDonald, he died in '89. What I know is what my aunt told me about it. Grandpa McDonald kind of got in a little mix up in Scotland. Killed a stag in some hunting oufit's place. So, he come out of there into Ontario and then down to Fort Hall, Idaho. That's where the Hudson's Bay was at that time. He was kind of a roustabout clerk to start with. And that's where my grandmother grew up at Fort Hall. And then when she grew up, they got married there. They had two children there, Charles and Christine. And then they moved from there to Fort Colville, I think it was, and run the post there, and the one at Post Creek. Angus was a full-blooded Scotchman. He come here with the Hudson's Bay as a trader. And in all his trading and everything else, he was always fair with them, and that's why they all respected him. He was more or less kind of leaning in their favor all of the time.

They are buried out here at Post Creek, my grandfather and grandmother. He died in '89 and my grandmother, she died in 1901, I think. She was part Nez Perce and part Iroquois. Her father was Iroquois. I imagine they must have been out here with the early day trappers and trying to get the religion to get the Blackrobes in here, because the Iroquois had quite a bit to do with that. My dad and one sister they was allotted on the Nez Perce Reservation out of Lapwai, Idaho, and the rest of them up here. Of course, with the Hudson's Bay Company they were born in different places. Now like my dad was born in Marcus, Washington, that was where the old Hudson's Bay trading post was there, that my granddad took care of. And an uncle of mine was born over here on the Dearborn River in Montana.

Charlie McDonald's
grandparents.

Top:
Angus McDonald

Bottom:
Catherine McDonald

Source: Toole Archives,
Mansfield Library,
University of Montana,
Missoula,
photographs 77-289 and
83-93.

I suppose they were on the buffalo hunt. And I imagine they stayed there for the winter and that's where he was born. And Duncan, the oldest of my dad's brothers, he was born here on Post Creek in '49, I think. And my aunt Maggie — I don't remember if she was born there or she was born at Marcus. But they were scattered out, where ever he happened to be.

My grandmother, she would just take her pack string and head from one place to the other. My aunt, just before she died was telling us about they left here to go to Marcus, Washington. That's up in the north end there around Colville, Kettle Falls. Anyhow, they had all the young horses. She took all the kids. My dad and brother Angus were just kids, they rode double. Tom, the one who was born on the Dearborn was a bigger boy. They got down to Plains, and they had quite a time catching their horses there. So, she said they had to make a hair rope, and Tom would rope the horses for this old helper they had.

So, then they got down to what they called Thompson Prairie. She never called it Thompson Falls. She always called it Thompson Prairie. They got down there and it was getting late, so they camped there. So, while they were there, there was an Indian and his wife a foot going down that lower country. So, he helped them pack up in the morning and then he would tell them where to camp, and he'd fish down the river going on down to their camp. And when they got to Sand Point, Idaho, she knew some old-time trader there, and he gave them a little credit there. And then they went to a place they called Peone Prairie, I think, and there was an old trader there and he give 'em stuff enough so she could get on up to Marcus with all these kids.

A few years back, my other sister and I were down at Omak, Washington. And we have some way off distant cousin down there, from the Finan McDonald family. And she was doing some work for an old retired judge in Okanagan, Washington. So, we went down there with her. She was making a lot of his stuff and putting 'em into a book form for him. And he had a basement pret' near as big as this whole house just full of historical stuff. And anyhow, he showed us a letter he had there, where our grandfather had wrote to my dad's older sister. She was at Penticton, British Columbia, in Okanagan country. The letter said that, while I am writing this, your little brother Joe is playing around my feet. And then he went on to tell them about different things, and he said also a lot of your mother's trips was not productive. She would just take off.

And then another letter we had, my aunt told me about it, she said there must have been four feet of snow on the level out there around Post Creek and through here. She said it stayed all winter, and she said, finally, towards spring, they heard plenty of roaring and somebody went outside and a big chinook wind was hitting. She said it never stopped until ever bit of that snow was gone. She had a letter from him and, in this letter to her, he said — it must have been wrote when the winter was on — why don't you get the boys to chop brush to feed the stock, because that's where the company saved their horses in 1845. Ed, my brother had a copy of that, she copied that down. And then when he passed away I don't know what happened to it.

My Aunt Maggie that lived over in Nirada, she used to do a lot of buckskin work, gloves, mugs, and jackets and then ever once in a while she would fix some woman's fur coat. And then she made a couple of fur coats herself. She used to set by the fireplace. She'd be working on something, and tell us something about how they took care of the furs or what they done with them. But you know then when you're young, that just goes in one ear and out the other. And a lot of it now, I wish that I had paid attention, because ain't many of us that knows anything left about our family. She was always together about telling us things.

You see my dad and Christine was allotted down there in Idaho on the Nez Perce Reservation. She always lived there. And then her family was raised there. Her husband had the mail ride, pulled a team and buggy from Spaulding to Lewiston. He had that for years. And my older sister and brother, they were first supposed to be allotted there, and then my dad changed it and had them brought up here. That's how we had enough rights that we could of been either place, I guess. But he was the only one who was allotted down there. My parents had just a little ranch at Post Creek, and we raised a lot of horses and cattle. Just like about what the rest of them did.

This uncle that over there at Nirada [Angus P. McDonald] — I never found out until last year. I knew he was an Okanagan Indian. What came out when the enrollment was on, the Kootenais adopted him. And for a long time, he was pretty influential with the tribe. He used to have a den, a room pret' near as big as this, the house was a twelve room house. But he had a den. He had a mattress, and a coyote robe that he would slap on and he always had his lamp by him, and then his wall, he had more literature up there. A lot of this high class stuff, had lots, and lots of old Indian ax and thing, and I don't know what ever happened to all that stuff. And he was quite a reader, but his main downfall, he was quite a drinking man. He would go on a drunk, and he was on one for a month. He never bought whiskey by the bottle, he bought it by the case. And that's one thing that helped break him, besides the crash.

My Aunt Maggie would be sitting down by the fireplace, maybe making moccasins or gloves or something. Our cousin Tom — we called him Kootenai Tom — would be on the floor leaning against her, and then when she passed away she willed her place to him. And he was with her a lot. He's got — I know he's got some awful nice antiques up there. He's got a hair braided bridle, black and white hair, made in Deer Lodge. Years ago, when I was a kid, why we'd ask, "Where's so and so?" I would say, "Oh, he's over there making hair bridles." You know what they meant then, he was in the pen. And he's got that there and that thing must be over a hundred years old. There's a lot of other stuff. He's got a nice little room set up there with his antiques in it.

The Deschamps Family

My Grandpa Deschamps, on my mother's side, come into Virginia City when he was about twelve, thirteen years old. Two old Mexican packers brought him in there. And I think his folks was killed by the Ute Indians. What little history I can get, they must of come out of California in the gold rush. And that's why he come into Virginia City, and he worked his way up into the Bitterroot. He talked French, he talked Mexican, he talked Shoshoni, and he understood Flathead awful good. He talked very good English, but he never did learn anything about read and write. He used to pick up the paper every once in a while, there would be something about the vigilantes, and he'd want us to read it to him, and he would tell us what he knew about it. But, it's too bad we never took that stuff down.

My grandma on my mother's side was related to the Charlo outfit. But Sam Tilden told me a little about the Nez Perce going through, and that my grandpa Deschamps was with the volunteers that went to that Fort Fizzle, out of Lolo. And he said, Joseph wasn't wanting to fight anybody. He said, they watched him from their fort, they went up over the top of this little mountain right in back of them, and back down into the bottom. I guess that's why they call it Fort Fizzle. And all them old volunteers, Alex Matt, my grandpa Deschamps, and I suppose some of the DuMontiers, all them old timers. Just about two or three years before my granddad died, damn if he didn't get a pension from the army. And, up at Ronan, a guy running, taking care of, the cemetery told me he had some veteran stones there for them fellows. So, I went and looked at them, and they had my granddad's name spelled wrong. I wouldn't take it.

Chief Joseph, he couldn't help but being bitter. The first thing was, if the army hadn't chased him clear across Idaho and all of Montana, if they had let him go, there would have been just a very, very few shots fired, because he was not a warrior as a lot of these newspapers claim, Chief Joseph's a warrior. He wasn't. He was a man trying to protect his people and live up to what he promised his dad. If they had left him alone, there would have been never any shots fired.

I think in 1877, that Charlo sent a word to Chief Joseph, he didn't want any trouble with them going through. And if there was any trouble, he'd have to protect the people that was in the Bitterroot, whites and Indian. There's two things about Charlo, that they always said. First place, he always marveled at the thing he said, he never had no white man's blood on his hands. And he protected 'em, and then they turned right around with the help of [James Garfield] made the treaty, why that's when he claimed that his name was forged, that he never signed no. And the first was to let them look at the Jocko Valley, and this country, and then they thought they could have part of theirs back, as near as I understood it. Well that was reneged all together. And Arlee moved down, I think in the '70s, and Charlo never moved until '91. Arlee's supposed to be part Nez Perce. Charlo didn't like it, because he said his name was forged on it. But ol' Charlo, according to your history and everything, he was honest in all of his dealings. And that's why he got along so good with everybody that was in there. Then they took advantage of him, when they found out what kind of country he was in. My granddad and his family, he must of knew that they were going to have to leave, because my mother and all her sisters and brothers all born up in the Bitterroot out of Stevensville, but their younger brother. They moved down here in the '80s, and settled on Post Creek, just above my dad's place. So, I never did get all the connection there, but I don't know if my grandma Deschamps was a first cousin to Charlo, or their mothers were, how they were related, but she always claimed close relation to Charlo. I seen Charlo at Arlee once or twice, but not to go up and talk to him or anything.

The Bitterroot was a big country and a productive country, you could raise anything there. When the Jesuits come in, Father [Anthony] Ravalli, why he started them with a little agricultural stuff and there was a lot of game there, lot of fish, and a lot of berries of different kinds. It was a nice big country. And I never did ever get the deal of it, but my grandmother Deschamps talked a lot of Sleeping Child and I don't know what kind of country that is. I was never up there. But my grandma always talked about that seemed like they spent a lot of time around Sleeping Child. She always told that story about Sleeping Child getting its name. Said there was a woman picking berries, or something. She had the baby hanging on a limb on a tree in a baby board. Said the baby started crying. Coyote come along. He tried to humor her. Couldn't get nothing done. He danced. He'd sing and performed all kinds of things. And finally, about time she got there, the baby was going to sleep. Had his paw in her mouth. That's how she went to sleep. That's why she always called it Sleeping Child.

Of course, her dad, Rodgers I think, he was kind of a hunter for them forts. Cause she'd tell us different things about being away from Montana, into them other parts of the country. And, I remember her telling us about one time there someplace, her and her sister laid down on a hill and watched an Indian burial deal. I think they killed this guy's horse. I don't know what else they done. And they cut the woman's hair. And as near as we could figure, they must have been over in that Sioux country. But she would tell us them things, but hell you didn't think anything of it, you let it go in one ear and out.

My Younger Years

As a child, I didn't have hardly anybody to play with but Indian kids. But that's all we had to play with. And then course church days was the big thing then. For years, the only church we had was here [St. Ignatius], and they had a little church in Dayton. But on church days, that old campground by our place would be full of Kootenais. And some of the Finleys would camp there on their way to Mission, for the church. And on their way back home, why they would camp there again, that was kind of a stopover. Church days was big, awful big.

We lived out there in Post Creek and all we did was fish and play up and down the creek. And never had any toys to play with when we were small. You made your own. And I never knew what a Christmas tree was. We come to church on church days, Christmas midnight mass. And where there's Christmas tree, we didn't have none like that. And then we all make our own things, like bows and arrows and stuff like that.

When we were kids, these foreign priests. You could always tell when they were coming up horseback on the road. They wore them little flat rimmed black hats and jackets. They'd come to your house and then instead of talking to you, wondering how the fishing was or stuff like that, they'd start right in on you with their catechism and stuff like that. And said that if you didn't do this, you'd burn in hell and all that stuff. So, us kids just as soon as we'd spot one of them guys coming, we'd head for the brush, and that's where we would stay.

Indians in the fall of the year would go by our place [on Post Creek] with pack outfits and maybe 25 or 30 head of stock and their saddle horses. Then go in through St. Mary's and then they'd take a trail. I think it was the north fork of Jocko. And they'd come out up there. I think they call it Lindberg Lake. And that's where they did their hunting between there and that Holland Lake country. And then when they got all the deer that they wanted, their meat dried, all their hides, then they would all move back here.

And then, after we got older, why we had saddle horses to ride, and there was all kinds of them. In 1910 when the homesteaders came, you'd go out to Charlo in that country, on horseback. When you would be coming home late in the evening, hell maybe the roads,

Joseph A. McDonald, Lucy Deschamps McDonald, and children
(including Charlie).
Source: Joseph F. McDonald, Ronan, Montana.

Charlie McDonald and four of his siblings.
Top to Bottom:
Johnny, Charlie, Mary (Sis), Florence, Benjamin (Bennie).

Source: Babe Rose, St. Ignatius, Montana.

Charlie's father, Joseph A. McDonald.

Source: Ft. Connah Restoration Society, St. Ignatius, Montana.

Charlie's father, Joseph A. McDonald.

Source: Toole Archives, Mansfield Library,
University of Montana, Missoula,
photograph 81-0279.

Charlie's mother, Lucy Deschamps McDonald.

Source: Babe Rose, St. Ignatius, Montana.

the trail you took going out, coming back you couldn't go on it. There'd be a wire fence and shack there. It would be a homesteader pulled in there to set up his homestead outfit. And we was corralling a lot of wild horses then. We done a lot of damage. A lot of them homesteaders, we didn't know their fences was there. We would come around one of them turns with sixty, seventy head of horses in a band, and all running like hell. You just wreck, riddle their fences. But we just never knew it. Well it, it was I guess we was just living too easy life, and never thought anything about it.

My dad started a little private school for a few of us kids at home. And then a few settlers started come in, and then we had a little bigger school. My dad had a teacher come and taught us a little bit at home. And then I think about 1909 or '10, he got a feller going through to Kalispell in a covered wagon. And he taught us kids, my Uncle Tom's kids, and Carey kids was there, and Camille boy, and just any of the white people happened to be around went to school there for a while, at our old house. Then a some of them went to Ursulines, and some went to the Fathers. Old man Pablo, Michel Pablo, he had a school at his place. I think his sons, three of them then, I believe, and my brother used to go up there and stay with them.

And I went to school at the old Ronan government school for a little while. I guess that was my first experience in a day school, because our aunt took us up there. That must have been 1908 or '09. The schoolhouse was built in a T. I was telling some of the guys the other day, that was the first hot lunch program that was on the reservation. At that time, it was a lot of the old army rations like beans, and macaroni, and prunes, and that is what they'd cook up for us kids. And then we would go back there, and that is what we would have our dinner. And the superintendent had a cook for us. And then they had lots of cordwood between the school and the teacher's house. And then three boys would have to go out and saw up a whole bunch of wood for the school and for their house. And that's where the heating system was. And most of my playmates was the Indian kids when we would come to town.

My schooling didn't amount to much. I actually finished the fifth grade. The rest of the time, it was knocks and hard experience. I went to school one year in Chemewa Oregon Indian School, 1912, and came back 1913. And then I went in '16 up to '18 at Cushman

Indian Trade School in Tacoma, Washington. You went to school a half a day, and you went to a trade the other half. But I never did get a full year in at that place. That Ed and Walter, I think they both finished at Haskell. And my sisters, they went to Ursulines, I guess, and the government day school. That's about the way it went. But there was a lot of Indian kids that went to the Sisters of Providence, that had the hospital. They had a school too at one time. My mother went there. I think that burned down. Then the Ursuline nuns they stayed and they had quite a big school. Then the Fathers' boys, there was quite a bunch of them there. So, war was on and so then I come home and was figuring on going to the service.

The Sisters of Charity or Providence — whatever you call them, they were running a couple hundred head of cattle. They had a big dairy. They had quite a chicken ranch, and raised a lot of their own stuff. The Fathers had, they had a big orchard there. They had an orchard over there where that park is. They raised a lot of their own produce. They had lots of pigs, lots of calves, and a dairy there. Ursuline nuns was the same way. They had quite a layout. And they all folded, and I don't know what caused it either. And boy, they were putting out a lot of stuff. They even had the old flour mill running. Of course, that run right up into pret' near into the thirties, because Rod Arlint bought that outfit. They were going to restore that old mill. So, I was telling him one day, I said, "Hell, I sacked flour in that thing in twenty-seven. And we would have to weigh out the flour and then sew the sack. And the bran and stuff had to be all taken care of." Yeah, there was of course everything.

It was just like these butchers. They didn't call them cow buyers. They would come out of Missoula or Wallace or some of them places. They'd go around and buy up a bunch of beef, and you would take them from one place to the other until they got all they wanted. Then you'd trail them into Ravalli and load 'em out. Robert Ashley and I got into a deal one time when we were kids. We went with a guy up, I think about where Allard's are, and he was buyin' pigs. And he would buy a few pigs there, and we would drive them down the road to the next place that we were going to stop. One might have four or five pigs to sell, maybe two. Well, he'd put them into what he already bought, and then you'd just keep adding on as you go along. After we got all of our pigs gathered up, we would put them in the corral down there at the Fathers' overnight. So, when we got here to Mission we had, I suppose, thirty-five or forty head of hogs. Next morning, we drove to Ravalli to the stockyard. The pothole up on top of the hill, that was all open. There was no park then. Gee, they smelled that ol' water, and heck we couldn't hold them. They all went for that pothole. So, we had to wait there until they got their fill, and we got them on down to Ravalli. We were boys then, about sixteen.

When I was growing up, our language was English and then we spoke a lot, every day, in our house, Indian, Pend d'Oreille and Salish. Once in a great while, some Nez Perce come, my dad would talk Nez Perce to 'em. We talked English in our house, my dad would talk to this old cousin of his and ol' Alex Bonaparte. He'd talk Indian to 'em. We didn't have to talk Indian, because we talked English amongst ourselves. There was a lot of French, my Grandad Deschamps talked French, and, when I went to school in Ronan, about all there was Indian kids, part Indian, and full bloods, and a lot of French. Mission was full of French. All the Finleys, most all the Finleys talked French. Ashleys up around Pablo talked French. Then some of these later people that come in, like Lozeaus, and Greniers, and them, why of course they all talked French. Roulliers. When we went to school we knew a few words of French, but we forgot most of it. And I think some of them Morigeaus, well a lot of them in later years, they talked French like ol' Dewey Matt and all them, talked good French.

Everyone had a sweat lodge. We had an old granduncle, ol' Alex Bonaparte, stayed with us for years, and ol' Louie Horse Head, he was another old Nez Perce. They always used their sweat lodge. Us kids never made a habit of it, we'd go and get in, when it would get a little hot we quit. But my brothers, Ed and all them guys, they finally built a good one up there in. Ed and they used it quite a bit after they were married. In fact, I think Ed was using his old sweat house, not too many years, not to long before he died. Yeah, they all got used.

One boy in particular I used to play with, fellow by the name of Tsooee. Indian name was Frank Sooee, he was about my age, and I always looked forward to him when he come to town. And he was one of the boys that was killed over there in that game warden deal on the Swan River. I suppose you heard about that in your history. So, he was one of my friends. He was just a boy then.

Alex Bonaparte, Charlie's uncle.

Source: Babe Rose, St. Ignatius, Montana.

There was a lot of the allotments here that instead of translating the Indian name, they tried to spell them, and they are way off on 'em. I don't know how it would be, but they got them on the rolls as Stousee, but the Indian name is Sooee. A lot of Flathead words is a little hard to say. It's just like Beaverheads at Crow Creek up here. Their name on the roll at the agency is Calowahcan, but the real Indian name to that would be Palowahcan. And there is a few of them they did translate, like Chief Eagle. He was allotted as Chief Eagle. Big Crane, Big Crane. Just a few of them, but most of them they tried to spell out that name and it didn't work out. Now like on the Blackfeet Reservation and the Sioux they had a lot of peculiar names because they were all translated into the English language like Bear Child, Running Crane, Spotted Eagle, and all them. But they never done that here, just a few of them did.

Working with livestock was all we ever done, you know. When we were kids, my dad had cattle, and he had a lot of horses. My dad was a good horse man. He always liked horses, and he had a lot of horses, and he knew how to handle them. Because in '91 he took a bunch of horses, and he went up through Eureka, through the Crow's Nest and past Fort McLeod and sold his horses. I think he said it was '91. And if he hadn't had a letter of introduction to some big old English officer up there, because he had no inspection on these horses. So, they inspected the stock at [Fort] McLeod and let him go, because he give this letter to them from his father. Along about 1900, I think, then he took another bunch of horses up through Browning over to Lethbridge. And he always liked horses. Of course, we was all riding horses as far back as we could remember. Then we'd help with the cattle. And then when I got bigger we would work with these other ranchers gathering cattle. And then when I went over home [in Nirada country] — I say home, that's what I always called it, because I lived there so long — there wasn't all much farming over there you know. It was all hay land and pasture.

There was a lot of cattle then. And lots of times over there, I'd see cattle run out pret' near all winter over there in them hills. So, you rode a lot, in mountains, big country. Sometimes you'd be twenty-five below your place and maybe that far north looking for cattle. Then I always liked horses, anyhow. So, I always liked to fool with 'em.

Angus P. McDonald, Charlie's uncle.
Charlie stayed at his ranch as young man.

Source: Toole Archives, Mansfield Library, University of Montana, Missoula,
photograph MS 562, 12-24.

But then when World War I come on, why some of the Indians didn't go to war. When my questionnaire was called — I brought it here to Mission — and I went to the guy that was taking care of it, and he said, "I can't do anything for you, you have to go to the agency." So, I went down there, showed the superintendent, told him why I come down, and he called the secretary in. She started dictating a letter that I was claiming an exemption from the army. When he said that, I said, "I'm not claiming no exemption. I'm ready to go, whenever they call me." "Well," he said, "what did you come here for?" I said, "They sent me here." So anyhow I was put in then in Class I and was ready to go when it wound up. There was other fellers they claimed their exemption being a ward of the government.

I stayed at my uncle's ranch in Nirada after 1913, because there was a lot of wild horses to chase, and a lot of cattle. I always liked to run wild horses, and they had a lot of nice ones there, some of the most beautiful horses in the country. So that's how I got over there. And when I got over there, you know it's a different country than here [in St. Ignatius] — a lot of alkaline and sagebrush. My brother and I got in there at that place at night, and it was the first time I'd ever been there. I got up in the morning and seen them old bunch-grass hills and sagebrush around there and alkalai. Well how in the heck are you going to stay around that kind of a country. But I always liked to ride and I guess that's why I just liked to live there. There was a lot of game there, but we never killed any. There was a lot of deer, all kinds of prairie chickens and blue grouse, and stuff right close to home, and we hardly ever bothered.

I got in the last big horse roundup. That was when they were filling this Ninepipes Reservoir. My dad and I was after these horses when we started, and I went over the butte into Moiese, and he motioned me to stay back. And then I went up through the Moiese Valley and came out at the upper end, and, when they came over the hill, I had a fellow by the name Conko took 'em. And when we got 'em to the reservoir, and it was just starting to fill then. And I took across the reservoir, and we did let them go, and they run right back into my dad. So, he brought 'em down along the hill and the irrigation, then was just starting their reclamation work, and they had lots and lots of mule teams, and they met a bunch of them. And the horses got so scared they broke away and went through what few fences there was, and I think my dad got in with three head.

And this one little horse we wanted was a little bay stallion. He looked so pretty out there. And whenever he would see a bunch, why he would just take them and head right for them buttes. So, we got him, and he was a little stinking thing when we got him in the corral. I don't think he weighed a thousand pounds, big long tail on him. And he belonged to a McLeod up at Ronan. Had a big SM on him. But when he was out, you would think he was quite a horse. And then you seen a lot of things happened there. We seen a feller get his leg broke. Wild horse hit a fence or something. And I've seen ten or fifteen orphan colts standing around our corral after the roundup was over. Either the mare was taken with the horses that was sold or maybe got killed or got separated bringing them in. They'd stay around our corral for a while and then wonder off back up in the prairie. And I suppose some made it and some died. We tried to raise two or three, but we never could have any luck with them.

My wife's dad homesteaded right across the creek from where my uncle was. Her grandfather [i.e., father] was the sheriff at one time, and wound up in the assessor's office in Missoula County in the '80s, when he died. And her dad was part of the Rankin family. She was a kin to Wellington Rankin and Jeannette. And then her dad moved up into the Flathead in the '80s, around Demersville and Ashley, where Kalispell is.

And my wife's mother stayed with her dad. I think she was twelve or thirteen years old, and she lived with this old Sophie [Morigeau] at Tobacco Plains, up there out of Eureka. They would come from there to Demersville, Ashley, with her packhorses. Cause her mother, after they were down on the ranch there, if there was a chicken hawk or anything around there, why she was a pretty good shot. And she said that's how she learned was with this old lady Sophie. I think this old Sophie was a sister to the old Morigeau family. They have a big monument up there at — I think there's place there they call Sophie's Lake, too.

I helped 'em on the ranch, and I rode for different fellows around there. I'd help gathering my aunt's cattle and then feed cattle for her in the winter. The boys was small then, Archie was gone. And Angus was small. Then after they got bigger, why then I started a

Charlie and his wife, Achsah.

Source: Jim Halverson, Polson, Montana.

little place of my own, and then when Angus — well just before he went to World War II, he was running the ranch. He was about 19 then. He was a good one. And when he was in Europe was when that multiple sclerosis hit him. And he was good for a few years after he got back, and then it made him an invalid. When I was taking care of the cattle for my aunt, he used to come from school, and I'd get him to drive the team for me, while I was feeding in the winter. Then in the spring and summer, we was always riding, gathering cattle, or branding, or something. He was always with me, and one time we started to cut out some beef, we had quite a bit of cattle in the corral. He wanted to watch the gate. "No," I said, "you get in there and start cutting them cows out. That's going to be your job one of these days." He was only eighteen then. By the time he was twenty years old, he was a top hand, and he had a bunch of nice cows. Yeah, he had, when he got so he couldn't handle the ranch, he must of had about sixty head of registered Herefords, and I suppose he must have had a hundred fifty, two hundred grey cows and he had a good ranch started, everything had to be just so. But the niece [Maggie McDonald Goode] has got the old ranch now, and she's taking care of him.

My wife and I had this little place kind of rented. And then I got ahold of some money and bought some cattle. And then I got a little school bus and hauled kids, just a few kids. Things were cheap, but you could make do. Well, I bought a brand new half Dodge panel truck to haul these six kids in, for 850 dollars. Why, you couldn't hardly buy a tire for that now. Then they raised it the next year, and I took more kids and I had to get a bigger panel. I got a ton panel on a ton and a half frame, $1100. Eighteen cents for gas.

We were ready to move out. The older girl was ready for high school and Altie was just about ready. She was junior high. So, they come to see me one day, a fellow below me, and he said, "What are you going to do." I said, "Well, I figured on moving to town. We got to get to a high school." "Well," he said, "if you move out your kids, we ain't going to have enough kids here to hold ours." Well I said, "If you get a good driver, I said I would stay, but if you don't, I'll move to town." So, I put in a bid, and I got it. Seventy-five dollars a month, paying on an $850 Dodge. And the funny part was I bid on it, and I didn't have a dime. I know that. I said, "I'm going down to the bank." He said, "You go on down to my bank and see what you do there, and you stop when you come back." The fellow I was buying the car from was just walking out of the bank, and I met him. I didn't have any idea of buying it from him. He said, "Well if you want to buy a Dodge from me, I got it already fixed for you." I said, "You have?" "Yeah, go back in there and talk to them." We walked right back in, and he says, "How do you want to pay for it?" I said, "I just want so much for each warrant turned right in to you from the school. I won't even have my hand." That was the First National Bank in Plains. But that was depression days. You talk of depression you know. I know a fellow over home had six dressed hogs, and he was taking them to Kalispell. He loaded them crossways on his old Model T. And he took 'em to Kalispell, and he darn near had to bring them home. He finally sold them for six cents a pound. She was really tough.

They all got along now. Below us you know they started them relief programs. And that's where I was. We was scattered out. What the fellows done there, they trapped coyotes, muskrat, and mink. Whenever the sheepmen wanted a few men to work lambing or shearing or something, why they would work for them. And that is the way they got by. Some rancher wanted some fence built or something. They made it.

I participated just a little in the work projects. I dug ditch down in Hot Springs. I was only on it about three days. It was too far away to go. It didn't really pay. And then I could help them fellers ride for them, and the sheep outfits. But we got by pretty good. And everybody had a good garden. Everybody had their own milk cows. Had their own milk and butter. You didn't starve.

What happened to the Indian allotments was the sad deal. That was a lot of politics in that. First place, the allotment act, I think they should have been three hundred twenty acres, instead of them eighties and hundred and sixty. That was the first thing that they didn't do. Then the next thing, I think if there'd have been a way of freezing the allotments, we'd have been a hell of a lot better off. So, the people got their allotments, and the white man come in and he knew that there was a good chance of making a go of it. So, he would get ahold of this feller that guy and give him a big talk. He'd like to buy him out. Well the next thing the guy would apply for a patent in fee and, when they'd get that, why, the place was sold. And ninety percent of the money was never used to a good advantage. And the first thing his allotment was gone, and he didn't have nothing. Well that's that way it kept a going, and it's just like this, these [George H.] Beckwiths and [Stanley] Scearce and them fellers, they just get ahold of these guys that were ready to sell and they could get their patents for 'em and then, and that kind of died down.

They started what they called a forced patent. They give you an allotment and then the next thing they showed up and called you into the agency and they would say your patent in fee is here for your place. And a lot of them figured, well that was a good way to get some money, and they'd take 'em. I was one. I went down to the agency and they called me in the office. The superintendent said, "The patent to your land is here." I said, "I don't want it. Heck, my folks are living on my place." And I said, "I ain't doing nothing, all I am doing is cowboying around the country. Different fellows ride for. I'm not there half the time. I don't want my patent."

I convinced the superintendent. I walked right out of his office and I walked into an Indian who was chief clerk and he belonged to the Gros Ventre Indians, by the name of [Isaac] Hawley, and a fellow by the name of Mackenstadt, he was one of the clerks, the finance clerk. So, I met them out there, and that's the first thing he said to me, "Heck, you'd just as well go in there and sign that. It's already recorded in the county, and you'll be paying taxes on it." So, when they told me that. Coming from an Indian you'd thought he would want to protect me. So, l went in and signed it and got my patent. And I could've got a $4500 mortgage on it, and I wouldn't take it. I think it was $2500 I mortgaged it for. And I said, "I want to get it so I could pay it out." So, I worked all that year and I saved every dollar I could get. And that was right at the depression after World War I. And heck when I woke up, sheep wasn't worth nothing — cattle wasn't worth nothing. I was awful careful that whole summer. And by golly, when the fall come, all I had was Stetson hat I bought and a pair of spurs. I think [that] is all I got out of the whole deal. And I didn't know my uncle was going under that World War I crash. So, when I come to, why then right after World War I, there was a stretch in there, you couldn't get a god damn job no place. And that's how I lost my place.

First my place went to a joint bank loan account in Denver. I just can't remember who was the first one who bought it. The bank in Denver was a big real estate outfit. There was a lot of them around through the country then. I think they were called Land and Trust Company or something. And they had agents all over.

Well, then they pulled another one, after the Howard and Wheeler Act went into effect. If we'd have got that Howard and Wheeler Act in here twenty years before, we would have been an awful different reservation. Well [John] Collier froze all tribal land, no sale. Well, then the way they would get around that was through the BIA, and the guys that wanted the land. Why, they would put up these supervised sales. Just a damn few of them supervised sales ever paid out. Went for an automobile or something else. I think old Pete Woodcock got a little house down here on the creek, was about all he could show out of his.

But I think if it had been now, I think we could've had a big suit. I think we could just went right there with a good attorney and just beat 'em all. Now my aunt and uncle the same end was there. They had that old ranch over in that Nirada country. That was one of the big old ranches left. And when that depression hit, and then in '24 my uncle died. That was her brother, why we started then to help sell the real estate. All these pieces of land that they bought when they had the sheep where there was any water, why she turned that to the bank without foreclosure. She said she couldn't pay it, and there was no need for the bank having to go through the foreclosure, so she just automatically turned 'em to it. So, then I turned 102 head of cows over with my aunt's brand on them. She branded with a M bar. A lot of nice big cows. I think it was 102. And they sold them auction there at the corral right at the ranch. And they brought $23 a head around.

We started gathering the horses. And I must have held together about 500 head of horses — different bunches, different times. And there was an old guy in what they called Oliver Garceau received them for the bank. They took 'em to Perma and shipped 'em. Pandrey, I guess got them. A lot of beautiful horses. A lot of thoroughbreds, palominos, and everything. And they were credited $4 around for them. And then that's settled and then they're after the ranch. So, then the bank in Kalispell, Kalispell Mercantile had a big loan on 'em. And the Superintendent [Charles E.] Coe, the Washington office kept a wantin' them to come in and take their patent and fee out. They kept

Angus P. McDonald and Maggie McDonald,
Charlie's aunt and uncle.

Source: Ft. Connah Restoration Society, St. Ignatius, Montana.

Maggie McDonald,
Charlie's aunt.

Source: Toole Archives, Mansfield Library, University of Montana, Missoula,
photograph 81-0280.

writing and writing and my aunt told them no, she didn't want to do that. They did never apply for it, and they didn't want it. Then they would take her up to Kalispell and try to get her to make payments on it. She refused. They couldn't foreclose on the ranch. So, they kept after her. They'd go and get her and have her meet 'em at the bank. So, they all met in Polson one day, the bank's attorneys and the bank and her and the attorney that was helping her.

They wanted her to sign some papers. She said, "No, I can't sign them papers. I am still a ward of the government. I've never got my patent. My name on them papers ain't worth the paper it's wrote on." But she said, "I'll tell you what we'll do, if you leave us alone, every time we sell any beef we'll turn so much money to you." That was about '30, I think. My cousin that's over there — he is an invalid now, multiple sclerosis — he was just starting to run the ranch. And just two years — I think it was — before he went to World War II, he paid the last of that up, $40,000. She could've told them to go jump into the lake if she wanted to, but she didn't. That was her way of doing business. She said, "You guys leave us alone, we'll pay you up." They did. But they wanted the place is what they wanted. Nice water right, big meadow, big 11 room house on it. One log barn has 22 head of horses. Another small barn held about 12. So, everybody wanted that. The private water right on it. The things they were working on it was that patent. And I suppose they were working through the superintendent too, for her to take it. Just like they did the rest of them. I think she must have about fourteen hundred acres where the house is. Allotments, land they bought besides that, and they had all that Mill Creek and Lozeau country, where they summer ranch.

But as far as the hunting or anything like that, the homesteading didn't make much difference. Maybe go out and kill a deer or something, but it didn't bother too much. Of course, a lot of them come out here to these places and they were fools when they come out here. We lived in Moiese Valley for a while on my mother's place, my brother's place, and we had a bunch of horses down there.

Chapter 2
Swan Massacre and
Buffalo Roundup

Swan Massacre, 1908

The Indians was over there hunting [in the Swan Valley in 1908], and anyhow one of the old Indians, old Yellow Mountain, he wanted to move out. And this other Indian, I guess he kind of wanted to stay a little longer. And I guess the game warden [Charles B. Peyton] had been kind of harassing them about things. Anyhow they come into their tent that day, and I don't know what really happened, but then the shooting started. I suppose maybe the warden was a little belligerent and showin' his authority, and seemed like he tried to take the gun away from this Camille Paul, John Peter Paul's dad, and he wouldn't let him have it.

And old Yellow Mountain, Stousee, and his son, and Camille were killed there. Peyton was wounded. This little Indian woman [John Peter Paul's mother] said that she started to run, and I think she had her baby with her, and she was going to have another baby. And they shot at her, but just hit a limb, I guess, close to her head. And she turned around. I don't know if she grabbed a gun or what, and she shot this game warden, and he was killed.

So, then she jumped on her horse, and there was another bunch [of Indians] up at Lindburg Lake right in there close. She knew they were camped in there. There was another fellow with the game warden, a German [Herman Rudolph]. So, she got on her horse, and this German tried to cut her off. But her horse was faster than he could run. He was kind of angling, and she got by him, and she went in and told this other outfit what happened. And she got into camp, and told what happened. So, they guess they moved the rest of them back to this other camp. But then the men, I think this ol' Euse

Finley and his brother, and I don't know who the others was, they all went back to camp. And I believe they temporarily buried 'em there. Till later on, they went and got 'em and brought 'em back here.

They have a little monument out here in the cemetery for 'em, the tribe put up here a couple of years ago. And I thought, I imagine if you look into some of them histories. And then they had a pageant that [Bert] Hansen put on, out of the university, and I think that pertains to a lot of that. Sooeee was killed. [Bert Hansen, "'As the Water Flows': Missoula's 2nd Annual Historical Pageant: July 15-16, 1950: Dornblaser Field, MSU Campus."]

And then in the interview for the pageant, Mrs. Abraham, she'd kind of hesitate, and then tell what she knew. So, after it was over, I took John's mother over to the house with me, and we had dinner. And while we was eating dinner, she said, "You know, she forgot a lot of stuff." But whenever they'd ask John's mother anything, it was just like yesterday. She just, she never hesitated a bit. Tell what happened. So, that's about all I could tell you about that.

And then I think little Mary Whispering Charlie, old Stousee's daughter, I think she give 'em a lot of more dope from her mother, when they put on that play. I don't know, seem like the title of it is something about when the grass grows, as the river flows, or something like that.

The Indians still went hunting in the Swan, but, it was a long kind of a bitter dangerous thing, because after that for a long time, especially them Crow Creek Indians, they just didn't want anything to do with the game warden. And my guess, if another one of them bothered them in a year or two after that, I think they wouldn't of took any time, think they'd start shooting, and talked afterwards, because it was pretty bitter there for a while. And turned out, the Indian was right, and the game warden was wrong. We were on our custom hunting ground given to us by the treaty.

And [Eneas] Grandjo, and Ed Pichette, I think it was, the [Montana game wardens] caught them down at Plains trapping beaver. They took 'em into court. So, we had [George] Tunison, he was an Indian attorney for our tribe then on these claims. So, he went to Thompson Falls. And I was living in a feller's home over there in Hot Springs by the name of Sorenson, and he was on the jury. And he listened to it all. He says when Tunison got down there, he started to cite the treaty, and the treaty rights the Indian had. He said you never seen such a befuddled bunch of people. They never knew about the treaty. And he said if that went to trial, he said the county never had a chance in the world. But in the meantime, I think Ed Pichette died. So, it finally was dropped.

And from then on, why the jurisdiction different places began to show up. Like I was packing up at Storm Meadows from towards Striker, up towards Eureka, I packed in that country. A lot of moose in there. I didn't realize it. Nobody else did, but we had treaty rights to hunt 'em there. And that never showed up till the last few years.

Pablo Buffalo Roundup, 1908-1909

The big bend of the Flathead River was the last campground [of the 1908 and 1909 buffalo roundup]. The buffalo on the west side of the river was spoiled [wild] and had to load them into wagons to move 'em. Up above there was where the little ravine was where they'd come down, when they had the fence across the river, or on the bench up there. They had a wing fence, to throw them into that ravine, when they come down to the river. When they swam across, they swam into the pasture. Then when they got into the pasture, that's where they had the corrals and chutes for loading the wagons. I think it was two buffalo they would put to a wagon. They hauled 'em out of there to Ravalli. The buffalo that was on the east side, like from here up to Valley View and that country, over towards where Pablo lived, they were just like cattle. He'd drive them down with saddle horses. But these others got so spoiled, they would lose 'em every time they got a bunch of them. Allard I think got the contract, and he put in that fence and decided to wagon 'em out. That's what they done. And when they left, I think my dad said there was about 225 head [on this roundup], something like that. They took 'em as far as Edmonton, and then after they unloaded there, they took 'em, I think he said about 35 miles to Wainwright [Buffalo National] park. This was a natural crossing here after they put in the fence and made a good pasture where they could handle 'em. That's where they had their roundup camp right back in here.

The Canadian government bought all of Pablo's buffalo. That's how Pablo went out of the buffalo business.

My dad and brother were on the roundup. We got a long book from up at Banff. They sent it to my dad. [Thomas W. Jones, *The Last of the Buffalo: Comprising a History of the Buffalo Herd at the Flathead Reservation and an Account of the Last Great Buffalo Roundup* (Cincinnati, Ohio: Tom Jones, 1909).] I guess everyone that worked there got 'em. Everybody lost 'em or destroyed 'em. We lost ours. And here just before Mrs. Si Young retired from the Bison Range there was a guy come in there, and he had two or three with him, and he was one of the fellers that had done that. So, a bunch of the fellers from the Bison Range each ordered one. And when I went down to see if I could get one, they said the feller decided he was through. He wouldn't make any more. And they had a lot of pictures of the riders. A lot of the buffalo, even had buffalos swimmin' the river. Had [N. A.] Forsyth hanging in a tree where the buffalo surprised him and he couldn't get away. So, he hung up in a tree until they got by. And after that Charlie Russell drew a picture of that, him hanging in a tree and his camera all busted up.

There must have been 30 or 40 men on the roundup. Pablo had one bunch and my dad was part of another bunch. They were working both sides of the river. Freddy Decker's dad was one of the main ones, Joe Houle, Decker boys, Art Ray, Roscoe Murray, whole bunch of them guys. And Pablo's boys were on it all the time. Some of the Ashleys.

Chapter 3
Packing for the Forest Service

Packing for the Forest Service

I just worked the CCC [Civilian Conservation Corps] a short while. I skidded logs for 'em on the right of way, and then I went to work for the National Forest, and, when I come back, I didn't go back to work for them [the CCC]. But they had a big camp right above our place.

The first packing I done was just from our ranch on the fires. We had a big fire back of our place and we had to get a crew in there. My uncle, when he was a young fellow, he packed for, I think, the Canadian Pacific out of British Columbia. So then when he settled over there in Nirada, why he always had stuff around there. So, him and I packed the stuff and that was the start of it. And then I would pack the stuff for the sheep herders. And then in '29 the Forest Service called me and asked me if I'd take a carload of horses to Missoula from Plains. So, I went to work for the National Forests. And the first job I had, we hauled these horses out to Powell Ranger Station. We just using any kind of truck then, that was before they had really stock trucks. They had lots of old stake body and ton and a half trucks. So, they split my outfit up. Part of my horses went up in that Skalkaho country north out of Darby, and I went down in the Lochsa.

I had something happen there, I guess very, very few ever did. I had to bring a fellow out at night that was killed down there. Some of these horses I was packing was gentle, so they kept taking a few out of my string for saddle horses. So, I was going up and down the river from Powell with five head of packhorses most of the time. I got into camp that night. Well just before dusk, why these boys come into camp and they said the feller was killed. So, we started to get ready to go and get him. And here these fire fighters come. They made a make-shift stretcher and they brought him to camp. They had about a mile or so, I guess, to bring. So, they got him to camp and they wanted to know who had the short string. Well they knew right as well, it was me. So, they took him and wrapped him in blankets and they put these mantys [10' by 10' canvas tarps used by the Forest Service to wrap up cargo] and then they put these canvas covers around him. Laid him on his belly. I have a picture of the black horse I had, that was taken in Powell Ranger Station. So, they got him all fixed up, and feller by the name of Dan Lumpry and I brought him out twenty-two miles that night.

It wouldn't hurt me to go get a dead man again, because you know they ain't hurting. But I would hate to get one that was really hurt bad. Because any time the horse rubbed against a tree, you knew he was hurting. But the main thing was, I had an awful nice little horse I was riding that belonged to my cousin. I watched him. I tried to walk first. A lot of them trails, you'd be up above the river four or five hundred feet, and then maybe you'd be down on the level. So, I tried to walk, but I couldn't keep track of the trail. So, I just wrapped the reins around the horn and let him go. And he just walked to beat heck. And pretty soon he'd stop, smell around, and then he'd step up on the little rock or something, and away we'd go. So, we left Johnson Cabin down on the Lochsa, and we come up 22 miles. We left there about nine o'clock, and it was about three or four we got him to Powell, and the hearse met us there.

The guy got hit with a snag. They were just connecting up this trail, and there was this spring. A big log lay alongside of it. Part of the crew went over and sit down on the log and took a smoke, got a drink of water. Some of them hollered at him. They said, "Come on over and take a five." He said, "Just a minute. I just got two or three little places to go and I'll have the trail connected, and I'll come over." Just about that time the snag fell and hit into a fork of a tree. One of the forks broke out and hit him right side of the head.

That was my first starting with them. And then I worked with them that summer. No, in '28 I started first, I was out in Thompson River on the Plains. I was kind of a utility man there. I was on lookout, and I packed. Worked on trails. Done near everything,

Charlie's pack train.

Source: Ft. Connah Restoration Society, St. Ignatius, Montana.

telephone lines. And then in '29 was out in Lochsa. And then in '31, they started the Remount [Depot] at Ninemile then. So, I went out and worked that summer with the packers on the Remount. Oh, there was a lot of packers there. I don't know how many different places I went. I went out of Troy on the Yaak River, and I was packing up there some in '31 on a fire. And then I didn't do much again until '34 and then I went back to the Remount again. And I packed that summer at the Remount. They had all good stock trucks then. They'd take nine mules and a saddle horse in the trucks and then all your saddles and stuff. So, they shipped you all over. I went out to the Yaak country a couple of times. I was down in Idaho on the St. Joe, out of Plains down on the Clarks Fork River, and different things. And that was my packing.

The packers packed everything. They had what they called 25 man crews. They had an old cook that designed their emergency, for the rations. They had boxes, and they was all marked, first breakfast, your first dinner, and everything, on there. And they designed them, and they made them up in the warehouse in Spokane. So, when you went out there, and they called you to go on a fire. You were going on with a 25 man outfit. You'd load up your rations in these big boxes, they weighed about a hundred and some pounds apiece, and then you had your tools, shovels, axes, saws, and all that. And they were all cargoed up into bunches. So, you loaded them on your mules. and then beds, and different things like that. So, when you got to a camp you had a whole 25-man outfit there. Your crew, most of them hiked in. And then when you got to your camp, you unloaded all your stuff. And that'd get 'em by [until] the next day to get with their regular staple goods, like canned goods, bacon, and ham, and stuff like that.

A CCC boy took a picture of my string coming around the corner, because he got on one of my saddle horses. They were from Indiana, real nice little feller. Them packs on there were just even as if you took a string and run them across there. I was loading about 240 pounds to a mule, about 120 pounds to a side on canned goods. I think that we figured case goods at that time were about 60 pounds to a case, and we put four of them to a mule. I never realized what I was packin', but they had a plow unit there. And that was a knocked down plow. They had their own trucks, and a nice big team, and a saddle horse for the foreman. And that goes where they could with their trucks, and then they would put all their pack stuff on these two big horses. And their plow was all knocked down, and, when they would get to where their fire was, they would use that little plow for a trench.

Anyhow, one day the old feller that was driving the team, said, "Do you know how much you pack into a load." I said, "I never thought." He said, "You're packing near 2200 pounds for a load." But we had an awful big crew in there. God, there was horses and mules comin' out of Idaho, and there was horses and mules going from this way, and we wound up in that Lochsa fire packing mules from Fort Missoula. That was about the end of the soldier deal at Fort Missoula then, and they brought them mules out. And it was just a shame to see 'em. Each man leading a mule, and they were just groomed until they just shined. When they got down there, and they put 'em out with them packers for about two weeks, they were a sad looking bunch. They worked real hard with 'em. A lot the them got sored up. The fellers didn't take good care of 'em. But then in '34, I went back and they were more organized then. And then they were using planes in different places, to drop stuff, so it made it a lot different. And there was a lot more improved roads then.

And I seen a thing happen that at a place they called Meadow Creek up on the Yaak River. We had to go up a real high bank to get on top, up to this level. The trail kind of cut about 40 degrees or so, going down to the creek bottom where the camp was. The trail went up always, and then it switched back. I met a feller from Kalispell and he had a bunch of CCC boys with him. They were going to the fire. A feller by the name of Gus Thompson. I hollered, "Hello," at him. I knew him. And I think it was that afternoon, I started back up to that camp, and I met some boys bringing one of his boys out. Got killed. He got hit with a snag, CCC boy. The bank was just about as high as that. The trail run alongside, and I could see his arm and hand sticking up out of the stretcher. They just laid him on the bank until I got by. My horse just kind of looked at him, our mules. We went on and never paid any attention.

They had a lot of colored kids from Tennessee and Kentucky up there at that time. I got up on this bench, and I met a bunch of colored boys. And they were bringing out a boy who was hurt. The funny thing now, these mules never paid a bit of attention to this white boy that was killed and they walked right by him. But they got up there, and I don't know if it was the black object in the white canvas, or what, but, when I got pretty close to them, my mules got scared, and they broke all their ropes and everything else. And that's all I could figure, it was just him kind of moving in that canvas, and him being black. That's all I could figure. Because the white boy, I could've pret' near touched him with my hand. My mules never paid attention to him. But when they see these boys, I don't know, it just seemed to scare them, and they all went pulling back, and everything. That was in '34.

Oh, I got the mules all stopped and fixed all the ropes back. They had quite a bunch of them. We had a couple, three Southern guys that was packing there. Of course, they didn't have any time for them colored kids. We was in a camp waiting for supper. There must have been a hundred of them in the camp. An old lumberjack, you know, take a can a fruit, he'll take the corner of his ax and he could just open the can. I seen this little chunky colored boy trying to open a can of fruit and he was having a heck of a time. I was setting there on the stump, and I said, "Give me your can." So, he gave me the can, and I took my pocket knife and I opened the can for him and give it to him. Oh, he thought it was fine, and, when I went to leave to go back to camp, he asked me if I'd mail some letters for him. I said, "Sure, bring 'em out. I will take them for you." They moved them kids out, and he made a special attempt to get over to bid me goodbye.

I often wished I had got ahold of his name. Because them other guys, especially them guys that were the Southern race, why they just didn't have time for them and we had three of them. We were coming out of the Yaak River and were just on a level road like this. And we had to trail our mules about 40 miles to Troy. And this fellow with me was raised in — I think he was raised in Tennessee — and we were both packing, and this truck come along with a whole load of colored CCC kids, and they honked him that they were coming, and I started to turn my horse out of the road. Oh, he started cussing, "Don't do that. Don't do that. Let 'em go around us." Well I couldn't do that because the road was level as this and they would have to go out of their way. So, I turned my string out and then he finally did.

But the ranger, a retired fellow by the name of Byers, he told me after, when he was moving them youngsters out, he said. "If you ever go on another fire, don't take any of them colored boys. They are no fire fighters. Well, actually they are suspicious [superstitious] for one thing, and they are religious for another thing."

I noticed them boys always liked to work around our camp. We had a couple of hundred head of mules and horses in the camp, and a great big kitchen, and they said they got fed better at the forestry than they did otherwise. So, a lot of them, when they worked for us, they headed right for the forestry. And I seen some of them there, and I was watching two of them. I don't know what I was doing around the corral. But every one of them kids packed a Bible. They was awful suspicious [superstitious] kids. Everything scared them in the woods, I guess. But of course, you could see it, they had never been in anything like it. And he said, "They just bunch up on the fire, and you couldn't do nothing with 'em."

It was all whites who had charge of the colored crews. But the year before that — or two years before that in '31 — they got a bunch of colored boys out of Chicago, and they were really tough. Because, I think the story went that one of the rangers threatened one of them with a rifle, and another guy used a pick handle on one or two of 'em. But they were just plum tough kids, they were right out of the ghettos, and they would do anything to keep out of work. And they wasn't going to do anything. And they had them up at Libby for a while, but they didn't stay too long. They shipped them out.

But these boys from down in the South, like Tennessee and Kentucky down in there, they wasn't bad kids. I think the camp was above us, and I think they had 250 of 'em. Some of the nicest looking colored kids you ever seen and some of the funniest lookers. There was one kid there, he was just a complete bean pole. I never seen a kid so skinny as he was, and he could sing and whistle like anything. I kind of enjoyed watching 'em. Then I got into a bunch of white kids from Tennessee or Virginia — I forget which — down in the Clarks Fork west of Superior. Them poor buggers had never been out of the hills until they joined the CCC camp. And boy they were a sad bunch, they were all white kids. And then on the St. Joe was where I got mixed up with all these little boys from Indiana, and they were good kids. And the tough white kids we got was right out of Butte, and they was just as ornery as could be. But as a whole, they were good, all of them.

Down there in the Lochsa, there was quite a few Indian boys working. In fact, there was two bunches. There was one bunch that I took in. And they had a bunch of Butte guys, and Indians from Arlee, Fisher boys, and some of the others. We took two days to get 'em down to where they were going, at what they call Indian Post Office. And there was quite a bunch of them on there.

But Indian boys that they had, a lot of the forestry guys would like to get 'em, because they knew that they were pretty solid. They knew where the hell they're at, and where they're going. On that Lochsa fire, old Louie Arlee why they kinda lost him. They thought maybe he got burnt up. So, he come out the next day. "No," he said, "I wasn't lost." He said, "When that fire I see where it was gonna go," he said, "there was a little lake down there." He said, "I went down and stayed around that lake until it was over."

When you packed you got pretty well acquainted with most of the camps. Especially the cooks and the flunkies, because that is where you unloaded your stuff. And up in the Yaak River there is a lot of them old timers from Kentucky and Tennessee that come in there years and years ago, were tie packers for the railroad. I guess some of them left Kentucky, and they raised their families up there. We had a cook there. Oh, he was a go getter. I think he was a Navy cook at one time. And he had a camp. I didn't stay in his camp too long. They moved us out. But he was ordering bacon and ham and all that kind of stuff, and they couldn't figure out why he was using so much of it. But there was two or three homesteaders above the camp there, and he was trading these women ham and bacon for moonshine and home brew, and they finally caught up to him. There was a boy — I worked with him — was raised up on the Yaak River above Sylvanite and he said he was never out any further than Troy until he went to CCC camp, and then he got to go to Spokane. It was quite an experience to see them boys.

There was a real nice old feller that had lived up there for years. Most of them were staying on their place. We had one old feller — we had kind of an emergency camp which was about four or five miles from the main camp. There was a nice big creek there. They had a lot of stuff there. I had to haul a burned out camp. I got up

there, and I couldn't get away from this camp until about 3 o'clock in
the afternoon. And I had to take it all back about 12 or 14 miles. So,
when I got to where we're unloaded, the ranger says to me, "I hate to
do this, but I am going to have to try to send you back tonight. Do
you think you can make it?" I said, "Oh yeah, I can make it. It's kind
of moonlight, and the trail is pretty well." Well he said, "You can go
down the river here. It was on the north fork of the Yaak, and hit the
road and go down. You'll be about twice as far from your camp, or
you can go back the way you were."

So, they told me if I made it to this emergency camp, I could
stay all night there. I got there and unpacked and fed my mules.
There was an old feller there, so I went in there and stayed with
him and got up in the morning, and didn't have anything to eat.
And he had all these rations there. And I said, "Why don't you get
them?" and he said, "Oh you can't do that, that's forestry stuff." I
said, "That's what it's for." I broke open a bunch of them emergency
things. I got out bacon, jelly, and bread and stuff and we had quite a
breakfast. I said, "You tell the ranger, I'm the guy that done it." Then
he told me, he just spent all his life there. He was an old man then
around 70. And he was just kind of watching it for 'em. He spent all
his life up there in them hills.

Met some pretty nice people, and then you would get ahold of
some who weren't so nice. We got a boss up there one time, on the
Yaak. We was on what we call Spread Creek, I believe — it might
have been Meadow Creek — but they sent a feller in there, the head
boss, and a guy was settin' down on a stump. He had a can of peach-
es, I think, and he was eating. And this guy walked over and jerked
'em out of his hand, and give him a cussing, and told him, that he
should have known better. He'd get sick eating 'em. He went on, and,
if some guy didn't look right to him, he'd just tell him to go down
the road. None of the other bosses liked him anyhow, he was such an
overbearing guy, and I don't know where he ever come from. It was
such a big fire — it was the Spread Creek Fire because, when they
finished it up that fall, it burned out of Idaho and into Montana and
into Canada and then connected back in Idaho. I think they said
there was 340 some miles fire line around it. Anyhow, they had three
crews, one working, one coming, and one going. And there was a big
fire down out of Heron, in the Idaho part, the Clearwater, I guess,

so they moved him down there. And a lot of these fellows would lay around in the jungle [hobo camp] there at Troy, jungle up there a few days and then go back there to the fire again. They just take their packs and go back in the brush around the water tanks there where they could get shelter, buy a little grub there, and have their little fires, and cook their jungle food, their stews and stuff. And by golly, they brought him into Troy to send him out. A bunch of them guys got ahold of him there. They would have killed him, if they hadn't got him. The sheriff stopped them. Some of them guys that they run out of camp. I guess they knocked him through a window in a little restaurant there. But they said they would have sure got him, if he hadn't got out of there.

During the 1930s there were alternatives when logging jobs were short. We had quite a few sheep outfits here. Had a lot of cattle here. We had about three big sheep outfits. That is, fairly big. They run about 2000 head of sheep a piece. Dan Polotzin over there in Nirada, he was Romanian; and Nick Lasco, he was another Romanian, he run about two or three thousand. And the Polson Sheep Company was right out of Polson there. And they were run about the same amount. And then Dan Moore and Hermans and my aunt and Grunds and fellers like that, they all had quite a bit of cattle. And down towards Perma there was a lot of cattle. And the Forest Service when they got to get bigger, why the Grunds was living in a draw out of Elmo, and he wintered about 600 head of mules and horses there. Feller like that they worked around different things that away, and there was always a little logging down around Plains. And shows you the difference, I got some old scale reports here someplace. I moved here in '45 and I scaled some logs up there east of town. We got three and a half a thousand for yellow pine and two dollars I think, or two and a half, for fir and larch. Now yellow pine they are bidding it in about 110 a thousand.

In '45 cattle was starting to come back. Like my brother up here, he had a little bunch of cattle, and god they used to make fun of him, because they said he had a rainbow herd, all kinds. A lot of guys went out on the shipyards, and he wanted to go. But he milked a few cows, and he kept gathering cattle, and now he has got a ranch up there, I imagine, if he sold it, it would be about a $300,000 layout. He's running about 150 head of cows and has everything built up.

A lot of the fellers said the old guy that stayed out of the depression, who were too poor to leave, and they stayed with their cattle, and their cattle started to come up, and them were the guys that made it.

During the 1930s around Libby, Troy, and Heron they were logging some for the Great Northern. A lot of tie hackin'. They had little tie mills. There was quite a few mills. Of course, they wasn't paying much. You could go to work for a logging outfit for about two dollars a day, but there was quite a bit. And still like it is now. I think old Charlie would tell you he worked for about $45 a month up in a logging camp. Now they get pret' near that much an hour.

The Forest Service packing work was just seasonal. You'd pack all summer, and when you moved your stuff in in the fall, you would swear you wouldn't go out again, because, by the time you're movin' out, everything was wet and cold. And then when spring would come, why you didn't have nothing to do in the winter but live off what you made. So, you had to go back. So that's the way most of the packers done. But then after they got the Remount organized, then they started this Prairie Basin ranch down there below Dixon. And then they had a crew that they hired year-round there. I could've went to work for 'em, I guess. But I was living up in Nirada. I had my two girls, and they were high school kids then. I had a few head of cattle. So, I stayed home. And I had a little bus. I hauled nine kids to school, about nine miles. So, I stayed home.

Major [Evan W.] Kelly come in and took over the head of the forestry, Region One. They bought out these old ranches at Ninemile, the old Lumphry place and Schaffer's, and they rebuilt them all up, put in a big bunkhouse, big cookhouse, lots of corrals. And then they'd bring their mules in. There were a lot of mules they owned themselves. And they would bring them all in there. And then they'd buy a lot of mules and break 'em there. Well, they had different kind of deals. Maybe there'd be a big trail crew someplace. And they'd have to haul grub to them, Forest Service trail crew. So, they would have them, and then they'd have a district packer, for one district, where you packed for lookouts, or maybe a small trail crew. And then they had what they called a blister rust crew. Them would burn a lot of this blister rust. They had big crews in there. A lot of the packers went to them. And then when fire season hit, why they kept a bunch around right at the station. And whenever they got a call, why they

backed their stock trucks up, and you loaded your mules right out
the corral into your truck, and away you would go. And everything
was all set up, ready for you to go. And where ever you were goin',
well you goin' out in Idaho, or up the Yaak River, or Libby, or Troy,
over towards the South Fork someplace.

When I went back in 1934 it was a lot more organized. They
had better corrals, better trucks. They had regular trucks then for
stock hauling. And they had a big blacksmith shop, with two or three
blacksmiths there all the time. And a nice big cook shack. Everything was fixed real nice. They had that then and it run pretty good.
And then they started breeding their own mules and horses down
on this ranch in Prairie Basin. They had two ranches there, runnin'
quite a bunch of stock. And then when they started using helicop-
ters, planes, why, that's when the Remount started to die out. When
I was packin', there was lots of places, the only way you could get to
it was pack strings, but then a year or two after, well you could drive
right up to them with a truck, because they had built roads into 'em.
Forestry built a lot of the roads, and then a lot of these companies
that bought timber, built their own roads. But a lot of roads in the
national forests was built by the forestry for fire protection and sales
too.

Well a CCC camp was quite a thing. On the reservation here,
they built trails all through the mountains, and they built roads, and
more things like that. It was mostly trail work and road work. Off
the reservation, I guess quite a bit the same. A lot of places they
were working around, building trails and roads, fixing up lookout
stations, and stuff like that. I think it was one of the greatest things
happened. I think if they had it now, it would be a wonderful thing,
because it give a lot of kids work. I don't know what it would cost
'em now, but, at that time, why I think the kids got $45 a month. I
believe — now I'm not sure — I think they give 'em so much of their
money, and they kept kind of a savings. They could go to work, and
they all had good camps, and good supervision. Had all their trucks
and everything. I think it was a wonderful thing, and a lot of fellows
I believe, would like to see it come back. A lot of these boys could be
back in there. The Job Corps up here is a nice thing, but it's such an
expensive thing. Their overhead is awful big there. I don't know what
they claim it cost to school a boy there. Well I think if they were out

on the same deal, kind of like the old CCC, I think they would do a lot more. See all through the mountains here, they had all these trails fixed, and then all the roads was all cleaned out, brushed out, and everything. Just anything to keep 'em busy. And then they also used some of them around some of these recreation areas, cleaning up and making them up. They done a lot of work. I think some of them got their clothes through a commissary at the CCC.

Here on the reservation they took everybody, anybody that wanted to work. They tried to get all the young ones they could. Seem like they took anybody that needed the employment. Like over home, when they started their camp over there, why I just happened to get in by 'em because they wanted to use the team of my aunt to haul the logs off the right of ways. So, they got me to drive teams, skidding logs off. That's how I got in with 'em. And then I was with them a while, and then I was kind of smoke chased with 'em for a while.

When you skidded logs you just had your team, and you had a big tong rig. You know what an ice tong looks like. Well a logging tong looks pret' near the same with the big round iron like that. You just hooked them into your log. And you started your team up and pulled your log where ever you wanted 'em. We just had to pull 'em off the right of way, and we had boys there to stack them for truckin' out or whatever they were going to do with them.

I had my aunt's team. I didn't have any. But they had two of her teams there. But that's all the teams were used for, just to pull logs off the right of way. And then they had a cat that done all the road work. Bulldozers in there, I think they had two or three of them.

Well on smoke chasing, why you were stationed at different places. A fire was reported to you and you looked on your map and it would give you the location of the fire on the map, and then you would head out for that. On the lookout station you had the — I think they called it an allidade — an instrument with a hair on it. And you had a big degree circle on your map. You had to report a fire in, and give the reading in a certain section, and the reading on your map on their lookout, and then you'd look on your map and trace it out on your map, so you would know right where you was going. And lots of times, if they wasn't quite sure, they would maybe ask for a shot from other lookouts. And then where all of them crossed, would be the exact spot where the fire would be.

In the spring, they'd have a forestry schooling. You would have to learn to take telephones apart and put 'em back together. You'd have to make a makeshift fire line and then you would have to figure out the distance around it. Then you'd have to read compass readings. They'd give you a reading on a card, and they'd set it way out in the timber some place, maybe a couple of hundred yards. They'd use playing cards and nail 'em on a tree. And then they'd have a mock lookout station, and he'd give you a reading. Then you would have to take that reading then and follow that in to there and find that card. That's where you'd locate your fire. And if there was a pothole you had to go around. Why then, you had to keep track of your steps the way you went around and back, to get yourself back in line of sight. There was quite a bit of schoolin'. And then you had to learn different species of trees, firs, tamarack, and different ones. So, it was good schoolin'. I did that for a couple of years or so.

After our girls got little bigger, and then I got to be smoke chasing right out of Hot Springs, why there was no need to be going out. I stayed right there. So, then I worked there in the summer and hauled my kids in the winter. And then finally we left there and went to Hot Springs, and then they transferred me up here as the field man. I did a little of everything. I took care of leases. Sold hay and grain off of allotments. And took care of fire fighters, and took them out on fires. Just a little bit of everything.

That was with the Bureau of Indian Affairs. That was before the tribal took over. Then after I went to work for the tribe, after they closed this office, I was a field clerk for the tribe and you had everything to look after. You had anything that pertained to the tribe, like once in a while issue permits on post or poles, or maybe a little scaling you would have to do. Go out and check on some lease land or maybe some hay or measure hay or grain. Just anything pertaining to the lease.

Chapter 4
The Bureau of Indian Affairs and Tribal Council

We lived up there in the northwest corner of the reservation, and it was all Kootenai country. I lived with the Kootenais for thirty-five years or better. My two daughters, all their playmates was Kootenai kids. So, we never paid too much attention to what was going on the reservation, and we kinda set by our self.

One day I come home to visit my dad, and he said, "You get your per capita payment?" I says, "No." I says, "They got one?" "Yeah," he says, "some are getting a hundred and seven, and some a hundred and eleven." I says, "Hell, I never knew that." "Yeah," he says, "you better go to the agency and see."

My dad's older brother and my name are the same. So, went down there and asked about my check, and found out he had it. So, I had to run him down, and he give me a check for it. And then give me hell for having the same name. I said, "Well, I tried to get it changed."

So anyhow, I come over to visit my dad. And we setting outside, car drove in. I said, "Dad, you got company," So he went out to the car, and pretty soon come back. Said, "Them guys are looking for you." So, I went out. I said, "What do you want?" They said, "By God, this Howard and Wheeler Act is going into effect, and we have to have a councilman from Hot Springs, and we want you to run." I said, "Geez, I never even paid any attention to that." They said, "Yeah, we decided you're the guy we wanted," feller by the name of Fred Brown; feller by the name of Jimmy Lozeau. He had allotments up on the north end of the reservation.

So anyhow, he say, "You go over to the meetings." So, I went over, and, "Yeah," he said, "you'll have to sign up because we're gonna have election in a few days if your're interested." So, I told them, "If I can do you guys any good, I'll run. If I can't do you any good, I want you guys to tell me, and I'll get the hell out." So, they had the election. Old Dave Couture run from Camas Prairie, and ol' lady Burgess [Lorena Burgess] and myself. And I got more votes than the both of them put together.

So, when we had our first meeting, why I don't know. First, second meeting old Dave showed up. And when I was on the council, there was quite a few Indians yet that talk, but they like to have an interpreter. And when I was on the council, I'd always ask the chairman to have somebody interpret it to 'em whether it was Kootenai or Flathead.

And old Dave come in. I said to chairman, "I think Dave wants to talk here about something." So, he went up, and he said, "I want to contest that election, cause Charlie ain't suppose to be in our district."

So, after he got through talking, he said, "Well, what about it?" And I said, "Well, I don't know what he's talking about." I said, "We went to the sub-agency in Hot Springs for anything we had to have done. If it was too big there, we went to the agency." I said, "We never did deal through Elmo and the Kootenais." So, they overrode it, and I stayed on.

Well, it didn't hurt Mrs. Burgess any. Old man Bullhead was kind of a subchief of the Camas Prairie Pend d'Oreille. He was pretty well upset over it. Ol' Dave, oh, he got over it in a week or two. We got to be good friends.

So, I served out my four years, and it was a rough deal we got. Nobody had money; we didn't have anything to go on. Right after the last depression, and some had cars to travel in, some didn't. Some had to ride the bus or get somebody to take 'em. And every time I come over, I generally have to stay with my dad and mother up here at Post Creek, or something.

And we did have one thing though. If a job come up, if it was a Mission district, Ronan, or whatever it was, we'll always ask that councilman to get somebody that he knew would want a job to do the work, not them. Well years later when politics got pretty big — especially on fires — a lot of them guys from the office would take leave time and go out on a fire, and even the councilman. And here we were setting there, there with nothing.

We tried to get Indians working on the fires, because they knew where they were going and how to get there. I like for you to have a big lightning strike up here pretty high in the Mission Mountains. There was two or three of them Pichette boys was alive then. And you could always depend on them. They'd go right now, and they're good in the hills. Them Kootenai boys was good in the hills. So, we had good luck that way.

At first it was all horseback traveling. I could come to the agency. It was thirty-five miles from our place to Perma. Then we figured about fifteen from there up to Dixon. We used to ride from Nirada to Dixon to my aunt's place, stay there. And once in a while, why I rode into Perma and caught the train to Ravalli. They had a local train then. But I rode all over the reservation. I rode horseback outside of the South Fork and the Jocko. And I don't know too much about it.

So, when I got my four years in, why I'd lost my daughter in the meantime. And so that I told 'em I was through.

I was on the first council when they elected under the Wheeler Act, before that you didn't have no voice. The superintendent and his staff done everything on the reservation. The first thing we found out was Polley Lumber Company was in with the forest supervisor, and we had all of our timber from down here below Dixon clear over to Dog Lake all optioned to Polley. And we couldn't issue even a wood permit on it until that thing was settled. And the tribe didn't have a voice in that. We got up one morning over home, and my aunt was running three or four hundred head of cattle. Got up one morning, and here was a bunch of sheep right in our yard. That was before the Wheeler act come in. But after we got into the Wheeler act, according to the act you had a right, if they passed anything, you had the right to veto it, and you also had a right to a hearing. And all that kind of thing come up. And then if you had any land you were going to lease or anything, tribal land especially, it was up to the council then to approve or disapprove it. Before that, the agent had all that under his own thumb. The same way with education.

I'll tell you about the sheep deal to show you how the government worked. My aunt had all these cattle, and we got up one day and here was sheep right up next to the meadow fences. Golly, we got all excited about it. Called up the agency, and they had rented the range to a sheep outfit from up here at Round Butte by the name of Johnson. They just ignored the folks all together. So, she got ahold of a lawyer, and they finally sent a grazing man and one of the other men from the forestry up there. Talked it over. I was there with her, and I said, "Well, Auntie, they want to know where you want to go with your stock." She said, "Oh, right back here." Well the place is right joining them there, and we used to call them Mill Pocket, a little forestry basin, and that's where the cattle always run, and that's where the sheep camp was. So, we talked it over quite a while, and finally I said, "Well, we'll just make the creek the dividing line." I said, "We'll take everything from the reservation line to the Bitterroot and this creek north and we'll take everything south." So, they went away agreed that way. Couple days come back, papers come, and they didn't have us on this creek. They had us on top this ridge. I said to my aunt, "That won't work. Them sheep and cattle going to go to that water."

So, we turned it down. It went on for a while and pretty soon they sent couple other men. So, I and a fellow by the name Thompson we went with them. We could see they're pulling for this sheep outfit, because when we got into where they had their sheep, there was no grass left. And this little grazing man, he'd keep saying there is nothing here for sheep. And a couple places you could see where they kept their camp and they moved and it was just as bare as this floor. So, we went on over the hill and into what they called Mill Creek and we begin to get into a lot of grass. Oh, then that was sheep country. So, we come on back down to the lower end of it. Spread our maps out on the ridge. Forestry man says, "Well now you guys can settle it here. How do you want your range." I said that's easy, we went over both ranges. You give us everything north of Mill Creek to the reservation line and in the Bitterroot, and they can have the middle pocket where their sheep is. Oh boy, they put up a cry then. Well, I said, "You guys left it that way, you keep it." And that's the way we got our range. Different things. You couldn't get a job at the agency. One time I went down there and this Mackenstad said to me, "We ain't going to hire any of the boys from the reservation this year for fire control." I said, not? "No, we are bringing everybody from the university." I said, "That's all right with me. I got a job. I can go packing for the Forest Service national." "Oh, you're lucky." "No," I said, "I just happened to get a job." And anything like that would happen.

The reclamation then before the Indian Irrigation took it over was the same way. They come in here with a different attitude. They had this idea that if you were a BIA man or reclamation man or something like that, they had their own crowd. They had their own dances. You didn't go to 'em, you wasn't even invited to them. Pretty near like the colored guy in the south. And that's the way we were for a while. And another bad thing got mixed up in it. The Indian Service and then what few businessmen come into the country and everybody who was a Mason got in with them. And boy she was tough. And of course, everybody went along as they always did, but as far as getting any help or work, that was out of the question. And then to top the thing off with, this Mackenstadt, he was quite a go getter. He belonged to every organization in the country. And Twitchel over here went to Washington to see if he couldn't get an appropriation through to pay for some of the Indian burials he had. He was a mortician here then. So anyhow, while he was in with this appropriation committee, he mentioned what he owed there, what we owed him. And he said that ten percent went to the chief clerk, Mackenstadt. One of the senators happened to catch it when he said that, and he asked him if he'd repeat it. And he said yes he did, ten percent went to him. So, he called a secretary in. And when the secretary came in, they got affidavits. They swore to 'em. Old Mackenstadt was in Missoula, and they never even let him drive his government car back home. They fired him.

And this same Hawley, that helped tell me about my patent, they got him about two or three years after that. So, them things all finally kicked back off. And it was the same way, we had a superintendent down there by the name of Coe. He set in his office, always dressed just slicker than a pin, white suits on, and a big flower in his coat. And by golly you pret' near had to have an appointment to go in and talk to him. Finally, when he got out of there, why then we began to get guys pret' near kind of our own thinking, on our own level.

I was one of the council, when it was first formed, that was in '35. We had one doctor for the reservation. We had one nurse. That's what we had. And our police force was an old Indian policeman. Paid about maybe five or six dollars a month, and they'd have to ride about 20 miles further to get down there to hold their court. And things like that. We didn't have nothing. The timber industry was selling dirt cheap. We were getting three and a half [for a] thousand for Yellow Pine, and that same thing now was worth 300 dollars. And now, since the Howard and Wheeler act went in, we become a council. We started to grow with it. We got more doctor help and more nurse help, and better law enforcement. It built up until now it is quite a big thing out there. It's just clear out of sight. I don't know how many employees we got up there, but the budget must be just over two million or so, just to run the agency.

When the Howard and Wheeler Act got in, I was put on the chairman of the law and order. A fellow come to me by the name of Roscow Murray and said his brother was in jail. He hadn't had a hearing, and they were holding him because he knew where they were getting some liquor. So, we had a fellow by the name of Peterson in here. So, I met him out in the street one day, and I said, "What are you going to do with Kia Murray in there? He has been held for three days now without a hearing." He said, "Oh, he knows all about where that liquor is coming from, and he won't tell us." So, I said, "I'm chairman of the law and order committee, and you are either going to give him a hearing, or I am going to take it up higher." When I got through talking to them, they turned him loose.

Come to find out, Peterson was one of the biggest shysters ever lived in the Kalispell country. We had a fellow in a little store over there in Lonepine who was about as near a reverend as you could find. He didn't believe in any of that stuff. Real refined. And Peterson laid his feet in the back seat of that car with an Indian blanket around him and a big Indian hat on him, and had Vallee go in there to try and buy a bottle of rub' alcohol. And if he had sold it to him, it would have been so innocent, because the man never even believed in that stuff. But I guess he didn't have anything like that. So, they went right down to Plains, and they pulled that on the druggist down there, and they got him for it. It cost him, I suppose, $150 and 60 days in jail.

Them guys were just the same as in the TV you see about these bounty hunters. They got so much credit for each one they got. And

Charles Duncan McDonald as a young man.

Source: Ft. Connah Restoration Society, St. Ignatius, Montana.

that was finally stopped after the Howard and Wheeler Act went in. We had a guy in here one time. We had a meeting and we had the liquor man. He was from Salt Lake then. He had all this western district, and he had one of the special officers with him, named Magee. When we got this meeting over, we brought up this guy's name in there, and one of the fellows made a motion to get him off the reservation. Said what he done, I can't remember exactly now. Somebody else got up and seconded the motion and then somebody else got up and said, "I'll go one better than that." And then they got it open for discussion. He said, "I just like to see him taken clear out of the service. If he ain't any good for our reservation, then he ain't for anybody else." Well this fellow argued with us. Didn't want us to do it, but we passed it. When we passed it, he said, "I wish you would send us a copy." And we said, "Sure you will get a copy." Well that started and we finally got rid of them.

Oh, that went on for all the time the reservation was, before liquor come in. Yeah, they used to catch them coming in on the reservation on Evaro Hill, down there in Frenchtown, down there by Plains, up here by Proctor, and all of these places. And they had this halla balou that when that was legalized on the reservation how bad that would be. I think when that was legalized you couldn't tell any difference than it was before, not a bit. We had that finally stopped through the Howard Wheeler Act.

Then of course, we got the revolving loans going, revolving cattle payments, and that got people started again. Then they got a lot of this grazing land back, that BIA had rented out to these other fellows. Like some of the sheep men had holdings that we got back. Couple of them we had to let go for a year or two to get the grass to come back on 'em. Then when any timber was sold — or anything like that — why, it was on tribal land, then instead of going into the U.S. Treasury it went right into tribal account. Which the BIA didn't like that very darn much.

Cause one day we was in the superintendent's office, something come up about some tribal land. Superintendent said to me, "Now, have that made out to the tribe." And the supervisor was sitting there and corrected him, and he said, "Oh, no, that has to go in the treasury." "Not anymore. Not since the Howard and Wheeler Act went into effect." Then the education, things like that.

Then I was the instigator starting the burial fund, we never had. They had a lot of them old agency caskets. This old Pierre, he got hit with the bus up there at Arlee, and he died. So, they had his funeral down here. Anyhow, when they got him up here to the cemetery to put him down. Why, these old caskets. I think they was kind of dovetailed in on the end. Just when they went to put him down in the grave, the casket come apart. So, by golly there they was. They didn't know what to do. Finally, some old Indian got it pushed back together. And another guy got a rope and they wound the rope around it, and that's how they put it down. So anyhow, when we got in there, I made a motion to get a grant set up for the funerals. At that time, we didn't have a heck of a lot of money then, we would set it us just like the county. If the Indian has any estate, why we can put a claim in against the estate for the funeral. If he don't have one, it would be an outright grant. So, the chief clerk, at that time [Steve] Lozar, he wanted it right here in the Mission, one place. I said, "No, that won't work. We got Indians in Camas Prairie, that chance to call the mortician from Plains, and we got Kootenai Indians up at Kalispell that live on the river there. Why would you want to bring them clear down here." So anyhow, we got it passed that any mortician would qualify. So, it went along a while like that, and then they raised it to $150. Then they raised it, and they made it a total grant after that. You didn't have to pay any of it back. Now they've got it up to $700.

In those days, the BIA had their own picks all the time for jobs. I remember, I had to change the telephone line up there in Valley Creek. I was working for them then. We had two scalers up there, and they were living in a portable scaler house, where the camp was. When we started to move this line over, this Champion said to me, "Now, when you get ready to have all them poles moved. You get Louie Pierre to do it, because Faunce won't hire him. He has a couple of white friends down there, and he'll go get 'em." So, I went down that evening, and he said, "Yeah, he would come up next morning and haul 'em." Sure enough, here comes the two guy's looking for the job. He said, "Sorry it's already gone." Well them same two scalers — show you how them forestry guys worked — they lived in that portable scaler house, and they come out on their own time and went in on their own time. And then they got one of them little speeders put on a track there, and they had to sign all their rights away to get to ride that home. Down here in Revais Creek, Faunce had a guy in there by the name of Rodman. He built him a modern little house to live in. Give him a government car to use. He come in and out on government time. Oh, there is a lot things pulled them old buggers got by with. There was a lot of people on the gravy train at that time.

The Indians who lost their land in the early years just kept moving back, moving back, and died off. A lot of them that's left here is living in these little housing areas. It's like an Indian over in Camas Prairie said, "One day we owned the whole of this prairie, and now they got us moved back, moved back. Now we are all along the edge of the timber."

The only bad thing was, there was no help for Indians. We had an old Indian over there lived above us there where our aunt lived, old Joe Malto. He had a little cabin, just about as big as this room I guess, and he had been awful sick. And my aunt Emma would take him stuff up there to eat. So, he had four or five little kids. One day my aunt Maggie said to me, "Go up to see how old Joe is." I went up there. He was setting on his bed. And I talked to him a little while, and went over and felt his head. I could see that he didn't have no fever, and he was supposed to have pneumonia. But he had little dishes set on the floor all around him. I could see where he was sharing with the kids. So, when I went back I told our aunt, "Heck, old Joe is alright. The only thing is, he has nothing to eat. What you folks are sending up to him, that's what he is giving his little kids."

I went over to call the superintendent, that was this highfaluting Coe. I explained the case to him, and he said, "You go over to the store and get $35 worth of groceries and have the bill sent down here." So, I said, "Alright." So, I went over there and got the groceries. It went on for six months or so. Finally, the fellow running the store said, "Say, when are they going to pay me for them groceries." I said, "They told me they'd pay right away." "Well I sent them the bill." I went back, and I called up. That same little Mackenstadt answered the phone, and I told him about it. He said you shouldn't have done that. You should have had the order beforehand. I said, "How could we get an order when they told us to do that over the phone."

Every once in a while, he would have that case. There was just nobody to take care of them. Just like when we were kids. I guess our family and McDonalds has helped more Indians. Well, we all believed Indian, more than we have white, I guess. I guess that's the reason. It was taught in our house. We believed in it. Our grand folks couldn't read nor write. I guess for that reason, whenever they were in doubt, they would come to us. I remember old Blind Michel lived in Ronan. I remember him and his old lady and his son. They'd walk down there from this side of Ronan. She might have bitterroot, and she might have camas, and sometimes they'd have some fish. At that time, they used to hook a lot of those native white fish on the creek. So, they'd walk down there and then my mother would give them flour or little other stuff what she could give them. And maybe they would go home or maybe they would stay all night and go back the next day. Of course, you always fed them when they were there. Or an old Indian would ride up on a horse, and in them days he'd never get off until you went out there. I can remember mom and different ones there, "Go out and see what old so and so wants." We would go out there, and he would ask for either her or him — my dad. And after that he would get off his horse and come in. Dad'd give him an order maybe at some store or something. And that went on for years. We are still helping 'em, because, ever once in a while, there is an Indian, after now that I ain't even working for anybody, he even come here yet to help 'em out.

My folks always had lots and lots of Indian friends, and a lot of them made it kind of a half way place going back and forth. A lot of the old Indians at the Crow Creek, they'd bring her [my mother] camas, they'd bring her bitterroot, and sometimes they'd bring chokecherries, sarvis berries, huckleberries. And she'd give 'em sugar, maybe flour. And once in a while, in the fall of the year, there was one old feller when the native whitefish was spawning in Crow Creek, why he'd hook 'em. He didn't spear 'em, he used a hook. And he'd bring her a bunch of them.

I had a grey hair one day come in here, and she was all upset. Her aunt was going to sue 'em. Take 'em to court over some will. I said, "Well, you got a copy of it." Yeah, she got a copy. I said, "You go get it." She said she'd been living in Minnesota, she married some Indian back there. So, she went and got it. I looked at it and I said, "Well your mother gets 40 acres out of this place. You got 38 acres and some tenths out of it. And the rest of the 200 and some acres went to this other Gardipe woman." She smiled and she said, "You know, I never even knew if I had any land." "Well you got better than 38 acres, and that is out here, and its real good property." Well, then the aunt called me from Spokane. She said she didn't get in on the will, and oh, she was mad. Then this girl told me then, the reason she didn't get in on the will, was my aunt give her a thousand dollars cash before she ever was sick. So, I think that is why she done it. Well it's been about the same, I guess, ever since.

It's not really giving legal advice. It's just something that you just happen accidently know. We've known Indians so much, know the different tribes. And now the Kootenai Indians are different. We're all on the same reservation. They talk a different language. Their habits are different. But still we know 'em all. We know their ways. They know ours. We have relatives on the Colville Reservation, Okanagon, Umatilla, Nez Perce, Shoshoni. So, you kind of get an inkling of everybody.

The tribe could use the money from the [Flathead Lake] dam to buy back the reservation land, but instead of buying all this arid land, they should have spent more time buying this irrigated land, a lot of this irrigated land, like the Pack River holdings there. Them kind of place they should try to get 'em back, they should have never lost this, in the first place. Twelve hundred and some acres. Well, they got two creeks down on the west end there, Post Creek — three creeks — Post Creek, Mission Creek, and Sabine Creek, and they all intersected there. Everybody fished there, old Indians trapped musk-rats, some trapped beaver way down there, a good place to hunt, good place to camp. Now we lost all that. Them's the kind of places, I think even if they have to pay more money, they should try and get 'em back. And it was just like this twelve hundred acres. I forget what they claim we got for it, after you take the portion of your share out of it, it don't mean a damn thing. And that's why I'd like to see a lot of that land back. You take that Ferry Basin, all that will ever be is a kind of a game reserve. But the deal of it is, you won't be able to get enough revenue off it to even pay your interest on your investment. That's where a lot of that stuff is, so you'd be better off having eighty acres down here where you could get something good out of it. And it might pay its way out.

Allotment and Opening the Reservation

I think if the Indians had had their own way, I don't think the reservation would ever have been open, for the simple reason they lived good. They had everything they needed, they had all the wild game here that they wanted. If they couldn't get it here, they went to Swan River, Thompson River, Little Thompson, down in the Nine Mile country, get their dry meat, their hides for their buckskin. Certain times of the year they had their berries, certain times of the year they dug their roots, for medical and to eat. Certain times of the year they knew when they wanted the deer, the elk. And then, my aunt said they used to make, try to make a couple buffalo hunts a year, one hunt they would go for their meat. She said the next one in the fall, I think they went for their robes and stuff like that, where the hair was heavier.

And I think the white people, when they come in, I think there was a lot of them was, give them the big idea that the reservation was open and a lot of fertile land, and they could just come out here and really make a go of it. Which was very sad, a lot of them come out here and god damn little ol' arid homesteads that you couldn't raise nothing on, their forty, eighty, hundred sixty acres. So, a lot of them fooled with it for a while, and finally they would give them up, and they would go back to where ever they come from. Once in a while, there was one stayed, and he had a fairly good homestead, productive, and he made a go of it. That is in a hard way. He got to work for the different ranchers, and by helping himself and his family, they'd get by.

And there was a man, and his wife, and two little kids. And they homesteaded 40 acres right close to where we lived. And he had a good job. I forget where it was. But he didn't have a chance in the world to live there. But that's what happened to just lots of them. They come out and get them homesteads and think they had everything in the world, and pretty soon they didn't have nothing. A few of them who got pretty good places and stayed up made it, but I would say 75 percent of them had to leave.

But then as I say, the Indians had everything. Up along Crow Creek, a lot of the Indians would go back into the timber in the winter. They had wood there, they were in the shelter there, the wind wouldn't bother 'em. Then in the spring they would come back out onto their places. Then everybody lived wherever they liked. They lived along the creeks, the river. They didn't live in bunches like we got now. The only time they come to the mission was church days. They'd come into church days and, and some had cabins and some had their lodges with 'em, and they would set them up. A few older people, I think old man Nename, I think old man Kakashe, a few of them, I think there was maybe ten or twelve, the Charlowain family, I think they settled right next to Mission, and they had their own places. But the majority were way out on their own places. They didn't bunch up like they do now.

There was this postcard of Joseph Standing Bear and his wife with Joe Dixon standing between 'em. It says on there, "Me, Joseph and Lucy opened the Flathead Reservation." And he never knew what he was doing to the tribe, but of course he went out in the world with a big reputation. But it was all of this is done through big money people getting on the good side of your senators and representatives. And then they promote these deals, and get 'em through. And that's why the tribe is having so much trouble now. We had so many jurisdictions that we had through our treaty rights, [which] laid dormant for years. Now they're just surfacing. And people are mad, bewildered about it, but it's true. And these fellers that keep complaining, complaining about what the tribe does, they should never blame the tribe. They should blame the senators and representatives. That's what was handed to the tribe.

They did say at one time that we were supposed to get 320 acres, then they cut it down. Then if you had real arid land, they give you a 160 acres. If you had good, productive land, they only give you 80.

And I believe at that time, there was some of them adopted into the tribe. I know they were. And there was some of them that was married white women. They adopted the white women in, and they were given allotments. My uncle Ed Deschamps was married to a woman by the name of Endfield. She was adopted at that time, and she had an 80 up there close to where Walter is. I think the old Couture family. I think Jess' grandmother was — I believe it was his grandmother, his mother — was a white woman, and she was adopted in, and she had a place at Arlee. Twin Demers at Hot Springs, his wife was adopted, and she had an 80 there, 160 there. And Maud

Larrivee, she was adopted, and she had a place up there at Dayton. So, there's a few of them. But there was an argument come up when they started to give out per capita payments. They wouldn't give 'em to them women. So, I don't know if they ever took it to court or what. But anyhow, it died out.

You had to have sponsors to be adopted, like the chiefs or different ones that get out and tell you who he was now. This uncle of mine that had that Nirada country, Angus. He was a half brother to my dad, and his mother was an Okanagan woman from Colville. So, I was looking at these records, and it showed Angus P. McDonald on there, half Okanagan adopted into the Flathead tribe by the Kootenais. And I never knew that.

But that's the way, and now they used to be a feller worked for us by the name of Gravelle, and he's from Whitefish country. Well he went down there and tried to get enrolled, and he couldn't make it. And he didn't have anybody to sponsor him, or verify it. So, after he's gone, and I supposed died, his half-brother wanted me to go down to the Fathers and look up the records of them. And this Martin had two brothers. One was four I think, one was six and one was eight; and Martin was eight. And they were brought down here and put into Fathers school, and they're listed as Kootenais. If he had that to show when they're enrolling 'em he'd of been enrolled as a Kootenai. But he didn't have them nothing like that.

Course then there's others. I had a cousin that showed up here at one time just before World War I. Feller by the name of Joe Gird. Never been around here much. Kind of a rounder, and he said at one time he worked for circus outfits driving these big circus wagons. Talk quite a bit of Mexican. He tried to get enrolled, but he could never do it. But still at the same time, he had as much blood as the rest of us.

It never started to change till after they begin to get their deeds to their allotments. Then the feller would sell his allotment, and the next thing it was foreclosed on him, and he'd have to move. So, he moved to where he could find a place. Some of them moved into the Mission, some around Polson. And that's the way the thing set. And a course through a lot of the productive white settlers, they could see a lot of this fertile land. So, they would get in with their senator, representatives, and the first thing they would get this guy to apply for his patent and fee, and he would get it, and then they'd buy it. And some of them didn't take care of their sales after they had 'em made, and others lost it through default, or foreclosure. And they thought they were, well heck three-fourths of that land was what you see around through the valley now. And then it kind of went that way for a long time, and then the white people would settle in here, and say, "Well, the Indian ain't doing any good for themselves, they ain't doing nothing."

Oh, they done some of the most silliest things you ever seen. You think of now, you just wonder about the things that happened. They issued a bunch of these patent and fees right after they moved the agency to Dixon from Jocko. Well they had a big blowout there about 1916. The Senators and everyone else who got that through, they come out there and they had a big day of it. I don't remember if they had a feed there or not. And they put on a big spiel. The women had to put their hand on the plow handle and they pledge a little something, and then they were issued their patents. My mother was in the bunch. The men went over by the riverbank and shot an arrow out into the water, and declare them a citizen of the United States, which they already was, and that ended their part of it. Some old fool from Washington, D.C., who never seen an Indian in his life, made up all kind of rules, and they went by it. And then they gave them a little button, but they were full-fledged citizens. I can remember old Philip Moss for years — Joe Dumontier, was another one — wearing that little button on their coats.

Well, then we get the Howard and Wheeler Act in, and, if that would have been given to us twenty years earlier, we would have been a great tribe now. Some of them disagree with me, but I could see it. [John] Collier froze selling of Indian land. Had all the administrative land that wasn't used turned back to the tribes. So, it went that way. So, to get around that, that's when they started these supervised sales. So, they would go in and make applications to the superintendent, and if it was approved then they would appraise the land and it was put for supervised sale. I think 80% of that them sales went up the creek. There wasn't many of them that really used it.

And, of course, the Indians before all of this happened they had lots of horses. Everybody had lots of horses. Some had cattle, so they were livin' comfortable. We never had what you call hard winters. They had places to trap. Everything. But, the promotion of the opening of the reservation, I think Joseph Dixon, I think he was one of senators that had big pull in that.

My ol' dad always told me the same thing. He used to say, "You got your treaty and protect it. And the only thing we can do is fight and try to keep what we got. Because if we ever lose this, they'd be out on the streets. And everybody knows that they've never got a square deal out on the street. We all know that, and the only thing we can do is just keep what we got and fight to keep it. Because they're still trying to get it from us." They're still fighting for Kerr Dam. They're still fighting for the balance of the lake. Them factions is pretty strong, and that's what we got to do, just hope to Christ that we keep our reservation as long as anybody is still here. Of course, that's the main thing about us, my family, I been raised more of an Indian then I was a white. I lived with them a lot, ate in their houses, sleep in their houses, I used to talk good Indian, good Flathead or Pend d'Oreille, or whatever they want to call it. But then I got away from that.

Chapter 5
Flathead Lake Dam and
Flathead River Fords

Flathead Lake Dam

The first, I know of the dam was when they started that Newell Tunnel. Caville Dupuis, I don't know if he was a chairman of that first old time committee. I think they had a name for him — Committee of Nine or Five, or something like that. When they started to do that, he went down there and ordered them off of there. And it didn't make, it didn't stick. So, I never knew much about it then.

And till I was on the council, first one on the council, and that's when they come to the tribe and said they wanted to build the Kerr Dam. So, then we agreed to the whole thing, that they go ahead and drill, do what they wanted with Indian employment.

So, then they got ready to work, so they had to have a mediator. That's when they got Archie McDonald, my cousin. He went up there, and he's a mediator between power and the Indians, until the dam was finished.

And unions come in twice to try to organize them. And a bunch of them come to Archie one night and said they gonna have a meeting. They said, "Shall we go to these?" "Yeah," he says, "go, go find out what they got to say." So, they went and listened to the organizer, and he didn't get much help. A little while they had another meeting. I think he had only about two, and then he quit. So, then it was built with a non-union outfit. And lots of Indians worked there. A lot of whites worked there. And whenever argument or something come up, why they'd call in Archie.

And I met a feller was assistant commissioner from Washington by the name of Deiker. And he come to the agency one day just about time it was over. And said that mediator done one of the most wonderful jobs that was ever done on a construction job. He said you know that dam was built with all that help, everything there. And they said they never had one bad upset there while it was going on. And I don't think they got a record of that at the agency. And then when they built the third unit, why he went back and work for 'em again.

If they got a union, it'd be just of been all shot to hell. They'd of brought in their own outfits, and what would the Indians've done? Just like about the same time they're putting that water tower at the agency, and got here a couple union guys come in and try to stop 'em I guess. So, they told them go and see the superintendent. [L. W.] Shotwell was superintendent then. They come and told 'em what they wanted, and they had two rock pillars there where you went in the gate. So, he said to them, "Guys," he said, "you see that, them rock pillars and that gate there?" They said, "Yeah." He says, "When you stepped inside of that, you was off of your territory." He said, "This is federal ground, and we don't want 'em here. And they ain't gonna be here." So, they left.

The workers on the dam had all kinds of makeshift camps. Some I guess had a lodge or two there, some had little tents. And my niece that lives at Polson now, Ruth Whiting, and that's Sam Whiting's mother, my mother said that her and sis, I think, went up to visit her. So, she said Ruthy had the most pitiful ol' camp there, but they were hanging tough in there. And then some built themselves little shacks. Then, of course they had bunkhouses for a lot of the men.

When they were building the dam, they had the big slide when they killed all that bunch. Why, Archie told me about it, because he had to identify all them fellers. And I guess there was no warning or anything when the slide give away.

Then when Joe Mathias got killed up there, why I think Archie said he was in a ditch. And that caved in on him. I think he said above his waist. Before they could get him out, why I guess it just crushed him in there. That's about all I know.

And then John Malatare was up on the side jack hammer working. Some guys way up on top there, they let a steel get away from 'em. And when it slid off, it come down. And John was in the right spot, and it hit him right on the top of the head and killed him.

Then we had two, I think it was two. One was a little Mexican. And I don't know, I think there was another one with him. And this car got away, and come down off of that hill. It was a coal car, and they got killed in there. That's about all I know.

Then there was, I think Archie said a white guy went off the end of tramway with a wheel barrel. But they never did find him.

I think they may have put in more safety devices. The chances are, I never knew it, but they must've had guys up there that was watching for them things. That maybe that's all they done. And I think all their hospital and doctor care was handled through quite a bit of the Polson hospital and stuff. I think Doc [Murray] Brooke at Ronan was one of the doctors they went to.

I had been at the place where they built the dam once, I think. And then we was there before they started to work, when they're startin' to put the crew in there. And we walked across the river on a cable bridge, foot bridge. That's about all I knew about it.

But my Aunt Maggie that lived in Nirada, when they were still here at the old Hudson's Bay post, she said, every once in a while, they'd go up there and camp. And she said that was a great place for catchin' big native trout. Said they used to be a lot of 'em there. But that's about all I know about it.

Fluctuating of the lake, water's up one day, and down the next. I remember old Peter Charlie used to trap beaver there above the agency. Said to him one day, I says, "How's trapping?" "Oh," he said, "I quit." He says, "One day," he says, "you can't get your trap." He says, "Next day your trap's way up on the ground." So, he said, "I quit."

Everything changed. Farming, agriculture, it made a change. The irrigation it took all of the main native fish away. You don't see any native white fish anymore. Cutthroat trout, the only place you can find them is you get up on these little mountain streams. And just a rare, rare case if you'd ever catch a little bull trout on Post Creek now. We could always tell when we catch 'em, because there were a cutthroat was, was kinda lively when he jump up. And there wasn't much pull on your line. But when you hook a bull trout, you could always tell, because he was solid when you hooked onto him.

We didn't fish for bull trout. We was always catching old native trout, and once in a while you'd hook onto a bull trout, but we never fish for 'em. The Jocko seemed me to have more bull trout in it. And the river, they stayed in the river. And Flathead Lake used to have a lot of 'em.

Cause there used to be an old Indian by the name of Julian, and he lived up there, just kinda west of Elmo. And on that north side of that Elmo Bay, why he had a place where he'd ice fish. Every once in a while he'd send some fish down to my aunt at Nirada by the mail man.

One day, had a bull trout and he had two whitefish still sticking out of his mouth. So, Angus was school kid then, [and] they cut him open. I think he said he counted forty little whitefish that was in him. Now there ain't too many bull trout there anymore.

Impact of Other Dams

It's a known fact that the damage the dams did to the fishing. When they built [Grand] Coulee Dam, Kettle Falls was one of the greatest Indian salmon grounds there was. And when the dam was put in, I don't know if the Colvilles was asleep or what happened, but they never got a dime out of it. Down them tributaries, like Sanpoil River and them, they were quiet places for salmon to spawn. They'd go up in there and catch salmon. Well they built the dam, and that took all that away. Up there at Kettle Falls you can't see where the falls was.

Then down on the Chief Joseph Dam at Bridgeport, the Okanagan River come in to the Columbia above that. Well, right I think down pret' near at the mouth of the Columbia at Okanagan, I think there's a place they call Monse pretty close there, that was a salmon fishing place. We put in a dam there that killed all that.

Our Kerr Dam stopped a lot of the fish from going up into the lake, and that all had effects on the travelin' of the fish. And Selah Falls. I talked to this feller by the name of Tilibis. He's quite an influence down there in Yakima. I took him out to Charlo. His wife had some inherited land out there. We got talking about Selah Falls, and he voted against getting rid of it. He says, "I told them guys we never would be paid for what we lost, or gonna lose." And he said, "All the rest of them went for it." And he says, "Now they can see it." And Hungry Horse quite a bit same way. Fish used to go up to Flathead and on up to South Fork. They can't get up there anymore.

Down at Selah Falls they try to put in the hatcheries, but I don't think they have them [so] they work. And any place that there's any dams, they're bound to make effect. They built the Thompson Falls dam. Well they used to be a lot of Dolly Varden or bull trout they call 'em. Fish like that would come up from the Pend d'Oreille Lakes. Jocko used to have 'em down there around Dixon.

I remember when old Charlie McLaughlin used to fish there at the mouth of the Jocko. Certain times of year, he'd go up there to fish for bull trout. Well, that was after the dam was built.

Well, after all that stuff got out of there, there was nothing to bring it back. Just like for years, Joe Ladderoute, [who] married my cousin, he had a friend down there at Bull River, and he went down there couple times with that guy. And they were hooking, snagging bull trout. And by golly they done that a couple years, and they closed that.

Same way with Thompson Falls. I think Prospect Creek comes in there, and the guys used to put two white rags on their leader. And when them bull trout was trying to get up the river, well that's where they'd throw their hooks in these big holes and wait till one of them got in between there. And they're snagged them. Well, they outlawed that. And they get between them places. There's nothing there to bring it back. The only way you can get it back is restock it.

Just like they're talking about Sockeye now. A girl on TV, I think she said there was four eagles showed up there, and they counted twenty Sockeye. Well, that's the thing. After they get so many gone, why there's nothing to replace it.

Flathead River Fords

Down there, this side of the old McDonald Station there was an old ford there the Indians used. There was an old guy, or not an old guy, he was young then. He was livin' in Butte. And he said he seen he wasn't gettin' any place, so he got himself a saddle horse and took out for Washington. And when he got down to that ford he tied all his clothes on his saddle. Got his horse, swim the river. And when he got him across, he didn't have any clothes on. He tried to get ahold of the bridle reins and he couldn't. The horse would run away from him. So, he said, every time I'd tried to run around him, he'd trot. And when I'd walk, he'd walk. And there I was with my clothes tied on my saddle, and not a damn bit of clothes on. About that time, he said he seen an Indian woman come on horseback. She was kind of laughing when she seen him. She rode out there and got the bridle reins and brought the horse back to him. He paid her. I forget what he give her. He said he was so tickled to get 'em. I got to meet the old guy. One time, I was running the bathhouse in Hot Springs. He was an old Irishman. He said he never got any further than Clarks Fork, Idaho. And when he come up there to Hot Springs, he was raising registered Durham cattle. And he told me that, he said himself. And right at that same ford, some of the Indians, Nick Lasaw told me, they called it wagon wheel, because one of them old Red River carts was found there on the bank of the river. That was as far as it could go to go down towards Washington, and they left it there. And that's how the Indians named it wagon wheel.

That ford was just upstream from Magpie. Before you got to the siding there used to be a Forest Service ferry that went across to the remount outfit. There is an old dump ground there. That's about where they used to ford the river.

Most of the Indians at that time all used fords to cross, but old John Eneas, his Indian name was Sonya, he had a ferry at Moiese. And about the time the homesteaders come in. And we lived down there at the time. And the fellers homesteadin' across, they used to cross there to get up around town. A wonderful old feller. Got down to Arlee, and he was shot down there, I guess partyin' or something. After that it didn't run long. A cable broke and it drifted down to what we call the Red Hawk place, and there was kind of an eddy in there. Floated into there, and that's how they got off, and they never did put it back.

And up there in the bend of the river, up there at the head of Moiese, there was a pretty good ford there. They used to even cross it with a wagon. And that's where a feller by the name of Pawn, I think it was. He was crossing there pulling a — I believe Charlie Kennedy's dad said it was a hay rake. And the rake, and he got too far over, and he went into that big eddy. He went into that. That's where his outfit, his horses, drowned. He swum out quite a ways. Charlie Kennedy's dad said that he don't think he was 20 feet from the bank. He said we tried every way to get him to come to us. Pounded on the bank and hollered. He went straight down the river for quite a ways and then went out of sight. But that was one of the best, well that ford there at the old agency. That was a good one.

There was a ford at the agency. I seen my dad direct a guy across there in 1910. And then along when they settled my granddad's estate, he's bringing a bunch of cattle from Nirada, and they forded them there. He said they only had a little short ways for the horses to swim, and they would be out on dry ground. A feller working for him by the name of Louie Brooks, said they don't know why he done it, but he pulled the bridle off of his horse and hit him alongside of the head. When he done that, the horse turned over on him. He said when they found him afterwards he had a big bruise or something on his head, and they figured the horse kicked him in the head as he fell. Dad crossed that [ford] quite a few times. And on the other side of the river, old Marcial lived there. He had a lot of horses. He brand with the crowfoot and he had a son-in-law Louie Charlowain, and they used to use that ford all the time.

You can have that ford where I told you about that wagon outfit went into the river, and then there was another one out there close to the mouth of Crow Creek. And there was another one up there close to Buffalo Bridge. Jimmy Michel was running the ferry up there. But I don't [know] just exactly the spots. But that's way most of them traveled. Now the story went this old Magpie that lived below Perma. They said he was altogether different than a lot of fellers. He'd just hit that ol' river where he come to it, and that's where he'd cross. He didn't have any fear of that river at all.

Chapter 6
Environmental Change with "Civilization"

When we were children growing up on Post Creek, no irrigation, and the creeks wasn't disturbed. There was all kinds of native cutthroat trout, native white fish, and a few species of rough fish. Had a lot of — not a lot of them — but quite a few Dolly Vardens. Fishing is changed, The pollution come in with the irrigation, and the native trout, the only place you find them now is up these little creeks, up in the mountains. Down in the bottom, the only thing we got left there is Rainbow trout. And according to the biologists, they claim that. — Well my grandson worked for [David] Harriman, well he said that the native cutthroat trout won't live unless he's in pure clean water. That's why we don't have 'em here anymore. And, then they introduced other species, like Eastern Brook, now Pikes come in. Sockeye salmons come in. And from where we lived on Post Creek, west clear to the river, there was nothing there. That was all big open prairie.

Oh, the fishing back then was real good. There were a lot of fish in the river here. The Waylan boys homesteaded, their folks did, about half way from here to Camas. And they used to come down here and fish, and, god, they said it was just wonderful. And then, I think it was Joe, and I think Bearhead was in. I'm not sure. They floated the river. And they had some guy from Washington, I think he was a fish man or somethin'. They got in that rapids there by Horseshoe Bend and boy he was just hooking them great big flats in there. He didn't even want to quit, I guess, for a while.

My Aunt Maggie said that, where Kerr Dam is, she said, lots of times when they were young and they wanted them big trout that's where they used to go to catch 'em. And then later on, why it got fairly fished out some. And then down there by Allicott's place and them rapids below there, they were good. I guess they still are. And there is another one gettin' towards Moiese, in the bend of the river there. And, of course, in here all that time, you had different kinds of birds, you had lot of prairie chickens, and ruffle grouse, and there was a lot of coyotes and different kind of animals. And it was quite a mule deer country. My uncle, Tom McDonald, told me one time that they used to go up there in the [Little] Bitterroot. And they'd wait and watch for the dust comin' off them hills, up there. It would be a bunch of mule deer comin' down to the [Little] Bitterroot to drink. That's when they'd get their bucks or whatever they wanted.

There was a lot of water fowls, different things, different kind of ducks, snipes, and find a lot of Bald Eagles, Golden Eagles out there, a lot of 'em, coyotes, a lot of muskrats, stuff like that. And now since everything is changed, we have altogether different, everything has changed, water fowl don't come in here like they used to. And the frogs and things, you could go around them potholes, you could hear them croak in there all the time, lots of 'em. You don't see them anymore. And them big green frogs that we used to catch on the meadow and some of them out west of Charlo used to have fried frog legs. There ain't any of them anymore.

Potholes was full of everything. Muskrats. You could go around to every one of these potholes and it would be just full of muskrats. And down there towards the buffalo park there is a place down there — I was telling them kids about it. I said we used to hate to ride there in the spring. There were a lot of these curlews there, and they would be nesting there, and you would be riding through 'em, and they would just fly down pret' near hit your hat you know. About half scare you. Now they're all gone. You don't see one. Over around home over around Nirada once and a while you hear one over there. And my cousin said there is a few nests at his place, but they're gone. Prairie chickens were just alive here, and we ain't got them anymore.

What happened to all those animals? The first thing they said done it was the chinks [Chinese Pheasants] come in and they run the other birds out. Well I know for one thing for a long while, if you get up above where there were any chinks you would still see pheasants and prairie chickens. And then this pesticide come in and I think that done a lot of them, because up there at home in Post Creek you

Charles Duncan McDonald, middle age.

Source: Babe Rose, St. Ignatius, Montana.

could set there by the house and you could hear them little native grouse drumming down in the creek bottom this time of year, just all along there. And now you don't even see 'em there. And over home, where her dad's homestead was, he had a cellar built into a hill there. I'll bet around his cellar, his corral, his barn, and even on the toilet, on each end of the toilet, he had a birdhouse. I bet there was twenty or thirty bluebird nests around his place. And just a year or two before my brother-in-law passed, he said there was one male bluebird come back. A little different birds you don't see anymore. And then we were just overrun with chinks at one time, now they're hardly here anymore. I think the pesticides done a lot of them.

And there was a lot of buzzards, you could get out on that prairie and see four or five of them buzzards, circling around. Why you knew there was a dead animal there of some kind. Then north of Crow Creek, Round Butte, Valley View, and that country, that's where the buffalo stayed most of the time on both sides of the river. Very seldom, you'd ever see one come on this side of Crow Creek. But up around Horty Reservoir they call it now, up in there towards Valley View. Why that's where they stayed all the time. Well, one change the homesteading made was the people then had to get rid of their stock, cut down on their stock. And then they try to get places for themselves. Just like old Pablo, that's when it started, his buffalo had to leave.

See the environment changed so fast. Post Creek was big. Right across from the 44 Bar there used to be a big deep hole there. And we'd go down there and swim in there, and then we'd swim our horses in there. Yeah, the whole place, maybe a hundred and fifty feet, where they would have to swim then way down. Them creeks was big like that, in the spring of the year there were real, if you had to ford one you wanted to know where you was at. Well after the irrigation went in, they cut all that down.

And over there in the Little Bitterroot, I drowned — damn near drowned — a cow one time, right where we watered the saddle and work horses. She kept getting in the garden, and different places, and somebody said, hang a board on her horns so she can't see. So, we roped her and put a board on her horns, and she run down there and got in the Bitterroot, and she wouldn't try to swim out, she was fighting the current. I had to rope her and dragged her out, or by god she would have drowned. Now there's just a trickle of water there, and that's happened all over. Post Creek's the same way. And right across from where our old house was, we had a nice big ol' swimming hole there. Up at my granddad's place, there's two nice big swimming holes there, and we knew right where them nice big holes was because you could always catch them big natives in there. The only thing we never done, us kids never hunted any big game. My dad would never let us use the rifle, he was always afraid that we'd maybe shoot somebody's horse or cow. But we shot a lot of ducks, things like that, with a shotgun or twenty-two.

There's bears along the foot hills there, we lived above where Walter is, but there was a grizzly there, but we never paid attention to him. Then above our old place at Finley Creek, every once in a while, there would be a black bear show up out there, but we never paid much attention to 'em. And over in the Little Bitterroot, there's a lot of black bears, there's still a lot of black bear in there. But after the big change in the water, a lot of your different berries is dried up and gone. God, you could ride along the creek — I remember we were kids, we would ride our old saddle horses in them bushes, and eat service berries, choke cherries, and stuff like that. They ain't there now.

And there was an old Nez Perce Indian lived at horseshoe bend on the [Flathead] river by the name of Allicott. He had lots and lots of horses. In fact, the Fathers and the both sisters, the Ursulines and Sisters of Providence, they all had lots of cattle and horses, and they run on free range out there, so they had to all get kind of settled some place. So, it made a difference that way.

And see about the time they had that was before homestead days. There was just more or less free range to all the Indians. Like old Michel or Nename down in that Camas Prairie country. They didn't know how many head of cattle they owned at one time. And my uncle and aunt in Nirada sold 2,200 head at one time. And Art Larrivee had the contract getting rid of old man Charlie Allard's estate. And he said he had, I think, 3,600 head coming over Garceau Gulch taking 'em to Plains, shippin' 'em out. And Allicott had lots and lots of horses, and I think when he seen he was going to be fenced in. Why he sold his outfit to Jim Parson, and he moved to Umatilla out of Pendleton, and that's his last place. He died down there. The horses went out with the homesteaders comin' in. People kept sellin' down. And then towards the last, fox farms and fish outfits got away with a lot of 'em. We had, my dad had, quite a few head of horses. I suppose, 100 head or so, there around that Charlo country when they homesteaded. Finally, we got rid of most of 'em.

Used to have a horse roundup that started at Sloan's. I think they got a golf course there now. When I was a kid, they called that Sloan's Flat. That was a horse roundup there for a while. Then they moved down to our place, Post Creek, and, it'd be about two weeks there. And gather horses all over where the park is now and down along the river. See just hundreds of horses in bunches. That would be about two weeks. The Indians would run wild horses in the daytime, and stick game at night. All up and down the creek, by our old place, by my granddad's, that was a campground. And the horse buyers would come in from the east, mostly from Pennsylvania. And they'd buy horses, and some of the guys would either take a slick ear horse, or he'd take his money, whatever they give him. That's what he would play stick game with. That would go on two weeks there, then their next move would be down here to the Fathers'. And then round up there for another couple of weeks. And there was just hundreds of horses and from Post Creek clear to the river at that time.

All the Indians that had horses did the roundup, my dad, my uncle, my granddad, and his sons, and all the Indians, different Finleys, and, oh, different ones. There was a lot of 'em. On the river there was a lot of horses, down there around Horseshoe Bend and in that country. That was old Allicott, he was a Nez Perce, he run a lot of horses. And, of course, the fellers across that river, I think just above the old bridge there in Dixon, I think old Marcial lived there. He branded with a turkey track. And I think all them guys along his side use to round up and corral at his place. Up on the Camas Prairie, I didn't know too much about that. That's about the way the livestock run.

When I was a kid there wasn't a tree there in the Charlo country. That was all just one big prairie. Now there's shade trees and everything all over there, but when we were kids it was nothing, but just were wild horses and cattle in there and lots of wild game like all kinds of water fowl and coyotes and eagles and things like that. Course a lot of them horses were winter kill there. I seen them old eagles when they'd be so full they couldn't hardly get off the ground. They would just have to run a long way to get a little momentum to get up in the air. The same way the coyotes would be so full they couldn't hardly run. But that's the way the thing was then.

Then they'd have — when more cattle come in — then they would have a cattle roundup. There's one would be on the east end of where Nine Pipe Reservoir is. They use to bunch there, and then way down west of Charlo, where they would bunch another bunch. And they would generally have two roundups. They would have spring roundup, when you would brand your calves, and the fall they had what you call a beef roundup. That's when they went out and cut out their beef, dry cows, three and four year old steers. And that's the way a lot of the ranchers paid their expenses then. Missoula Mercantile and all them different big outfits extend your credit all during the summer, then when fall come, that's when you, and that happened.

We done a lot of thrashing, and a lot of hay crews. Of course, it was all done with horses then. The hay crew would be two men on a stack and about four or five hay boats, and maybe a couple mowin' machines and a rake running. And then there'd be four or five of them outfits all haying at the same time. And thrashing was the same way, there'd be outfits all along. Everybody was raising grain and seemed to be doing pretty good at it. And of course, that Charlo country was all open then. That was free range, everybody's stock was out. They wasn't fenced in like they are now. And then they changed, now they got to raising more cattle, because they sell more calves. They never used to sell calves. They sold three year old steers and cows, dry cows. Now, they want irrigated pastures to raise good calves on, because there's a lot of milk from irrigated ground. So a lot of them went away from wheat farming. [Sugar] beets, they used to have a lot of beets here. And they got away from that, now they're all into cattle. And it's changed the environment, like over in Camas Prairie there used to be a lot of grain grown over there.

There's a lot of geese over there. You could scare them up on the upper end of the Camas Prairie and they'd fly down to the lower end and land. You go down there and scare 'em up and they'd go back up to the upper end. They had a lot of grain then, grain fields. Well now, there's mostly all them ranchers is in hay, and using combines, there isn't much left for them, so now there's no more geese that come in there. It's just because of the different changes is. When I went over to Nirada to live, from head of Lone Pine down to Hot Springs, it was nothing but a big sagebrush flat, grease wood. And most of that is out in the irrigation. Irrigation done a lot of good in places and a lot of damage in others. So now they're feeling the effects of it.

All of this was irrigable land, ever bit of it. That's why they moved in here. There wasn't any place — oh, down in that Lone Pine country — there was nothing there. Then after they homesteaded it, and they started to milk a few cows to make a living. They might have a ten acre pasture fenced off in their forty acres, and rotate that. They'd put their milk cows in five acres and then back. That's the way they done things. Conserve the grass and get what water they could. It's been a hard ol' game all the way through, and this one old feller told me years ago. He said, "You know, this is just like Colorado." He said it will be the third or fourth generation before they ever get this land paid up. And I guess he's pert' near right.

My uncle's place right there at Post Creek, just above 44 Bar where you cross the creek. Well, my uncle had them allotments then, and that's when the irrigation started. They had an old guy by the name of Stergus, lived there. He had one of them hacks, we call them a spring wagon. And the reclamation had his pastures all rented. That's where they kept all their beef. Whenever a camp wanted meat, why Stergus butchered it right there at the ranch and then he took it to where ever the camp was. Then the mules that wasn't working, that's where they turned them loose in them pastures.

And there was camps all over. There was one here in the Mission, and there was one out there at Kicking Horse, and there was one north of Charlo, and one there at Nine Pipe, and there the upper end of Moiese there was big one, and there was one, I think, in the lower end of Moiese. They had them camps all over while they were building their ditches and stuff. Then in later years some of them, they had one big camp in McDonald Lake when they raised that up. And I think they done the same at St. Mary's. Of course, Mission Dam, I think that come in in the late thirties.

A lot of the Indians never give a thought to the construction, I don't think. I think everything was running smooth and they wasn't much for irrigation and the ones that did have places, had plenty for what they wanted. Then there was, of course others, like Ed's place. I don't know if that was put in before my grandfather died or not. But there was a private ditch there that irrigated all that before there was irrigation. My grandad had a ditch up there above his place. He irrigated from his own ditch. And some of them fellers like that could get their own water. Well then my dad — I don't know if he had help or not when he started — and he started a private ditch below McDonald Lake, that's where Walter gets part of the water from now.

I don't think they ever thought the irrigation project would ever turn out to what it was. In fact, I don't think a lot of people thought that. I don't think they figured that, that change would come in the country and in the streams and everything. Just like Mission Creek right here, is a good example. You go down there now, and when I was a young feller here, all along up and down here there was swimming holes for any kid that wanted it, now you'd have a hell of a time finding a swimming hole. And I used to catch a lot of nice big fish out of there. And another thing when I was a kid, well the ol' creek come right down from St. Mary's, and it come in.

Well, after you go up towards, going up towards Callahan's, well just below that place is where the old main Mission Creek come it. Because when they would have this celebration up there where Gary Plouffe lives, that's where the one big celebration was when I was a kid. Well there was a little, there was a dam and a little reservoir where the Fathers took the water up over the hill to irrigate. And I remember us kids would, instead of being up around the celebration, we spent our time in the dam little pond, outside of going home to eat dinner or something. Well then after they put in the St. Mary's, why then they put in that big long plume in there, and they cut that clear off. And the Mission, the main Mission Creek from Mission Falls, it come down and it come in just the same way it come in now by, just below that Mission Dam Road. So, it made a lot of changes.

Mud Creek was another creek that they — well all of them streams that was under that irrigation — they took a lot of that water out for irrigation. Naturally it drained them down.

Chapter 7
Looking Back

And after I got home from boarding school, why I just more or less kind of cowboyed for different ones for a while, and then we started our own little place, and we had a few head of cattle, and then when we lost our girl, and then I disposed of everything. We moved to town and I went to work for the tribe. When we lost our girl in the reservoir over there. So then I guess I pret' near had a nervous breakdown. I think if I know what I know now, I'd have never left there. I would have stayed there. I just kind of threw up everything, and then we moved to town, and then I just kept working for wages after that.

I think, if I could have done it, I'd have liked to have stayed on the ranch with cattle. I think I'd have liked to stay on the ranch and built myself up a nice herd. Not a big herd but just a nice good substantial herd of one breed of cattle. That's what I'd have liked to have done. But first, it seemed like, you know, I guess fate plays a thing for you. First thing, when I was a kid, I had some horses that my brother give me. I had an old cousin, my dad's relative, a Nez Perce, he give me a couple of cows. I was just a little kid. Well, I lost both my cows. My brother give me a brand to put on my horses, and they run way down the Moiese Valley, and I seen them two or three times, and I lost them. Then in later years, why a fellow said to me — We were branding cattle — "Why don't you get started in the cattle business." Well I said, "I'd like to, but, god, money is hard to get. I went down, talked to our superintendent and he told me I'd have to have a government surety bond to get the money." There were two fellows standing there when we was branding said, "Heck, won't they take a note? Or somebody sign your note?" I said, "No." One of them said, "Why don't you try it?" I went down and seen the superintendent.

He told me the same thing, and I said, "Well what about Bud Brunsen, he said he'd sign my note." "Oh," he said, "if you can get Bud to sign your note, I don't care who you get, it is alright."

So, I got a bunch of cattle, and that deal, I had quite a time, they didn't build up like they should've. I can't remember what happened. And then we lost our girl and I sold all the cattle we had. Had a nice little bunch. And then I got started in another bunch of cattle. And I had them left with a feller at Perma. The feller accidently left his cow — I think they were drunk when they were driving them, because they left his cow and a calf and a yearling. Finally, he run a bunch of cattle and told me to just leave them there, "I'll take care of 'em for you." I was working over here. So, I'd pay him for feeding them. By golly, I built up a little bunch again. So, he died. A feller who used to help him a lot, when I went to the funeral, he said, "I got your cows at home." I said, "You have?" "Yeah, I took them up to my place. Leave them up with my bunch, and I'll keep them for you." So, by golly, I started another little bunch of cattle. By golly, they built up. I must have had about 25 or 30 head of cattle from that little bunch. And a tragedy hit that time. He was running about 450 head of cattle. And he was quite a friend of mine. I used to go down and help him when he branded and everything. Just him and his mother and his aunt lived together. A cousin of mine that lived in Nirada, she was divorcing her husband, and she got to goin' with him. So anyhow, we was gathering the cattle and he was helping 'em ride, so that evening when we got ready to go home, I said, "Well Jim, I guess we better pull out. I got to come back to Mission." He said, "Well, Margaret is going to take me home."

So, I kind of laughed and went, and I took his saddle out of my car. And he called me up the next day, happy as could be: "You know, I finally found a girl I like. She can ride as good as I can, and that is what I wanted." She had a bunch of cattle, and they got to going together, and she moved his [her] cattle down with his. And his aunt was just ferocious. She didn't like her. She didn't think too much of the deal. He and his aunt kind of got on the outs. His mother passed away in the meantime. So anyhow, it went on like that for about a year or two. And I was supposed to help 'em move her cattle back on her range. Anyhow, I got a call one night. Said they were both dead. They went over Big Draw, Clark ranch, and found 'em both. She was shot right here. It looked like he walked right up alongside of her and kind of laid himself back against her hip and killed himself. They never did really get right down to it. All the coroner said that night when they got there — they had been there for four or five days in July — and all he said, he threw up his hands and said murder and suicide. Well, I seen the pictures afterwards and I know darn well he never done it. Because there was a rifle laying on the ground and a little sixshooter right close to where he is. Well, the FBI told me after, "You know I will never take another coroner's word." Because the gun underneath was laying next on the ground there were still fingerprints on it, if they've looked. Well anyhow, we got rid of that little bunch of cattle then. Two deaths caused all that. Well then, I brought a little bunch over here. I didn't have a place. It was kind of hard to get a place, so I sold them all. I guess I just wasn't made for a stockman. I had a lot of bad luck.

And then when we got over here, then I bought this place. As everybody says, if I sold out here tomorrow or the next day, I'd move back to Hot Springs, because that's where all my old friends are. And there is third and fourth generation on a lot of them old places over there where there ain't here.

I didn't learn too much about working with cattle from the Indians because there was just a very few Indians that had cattle. They were all horse people. If he did have a bunch of cattle, he might let all the grass go to the horses before the cows got there. All the Indians around here, they all had a lot of horses. That's why we had such big roundups all the time.

The most of the stuff that I learned from the Indian was just more or less how to take care of yourself and how to live. And you would use to know different fruits that we could eat, berries we could eat, and the ones we shouldn't eat. And learn how to protect yourself if you was out in a storm or camping out anyplace, or something like that. Just like an Indian child — you very seldom ever hear of an Indian child drowning — you very, very seldom ever hear of an Indian child gettin' burnt. They'd have a campfire there where they done their cooking, or maybe they'd have a fire in the lodge. But they were taught right from the babies up that they wasn't supposed to be at them places where there was any danger. And that's where you learned a lot of that stuff. And you always learned about the birds and things. You'd be along a creek and you would hear a certain bird. I'll tell you what he was and what his habits were and everything. Just like the other day, it was real cloudy here, kind of foggy. And I heard a bunch of geese going over.

And there was an Indian in Arlee, Jerome Vanderburg, and he was working for me in the commodities one day, and I don't know it come up foggy like that. And he said, "You know this is the time the geese like to fly." I said, "How come?" He said, "They get a bunch of fog where eagles or anything can't get at 'em." And when I was walking out there the other day, and it was foggy and I heard them geese, and I thought of him right away. By golly, it was true, because you couldn't see 'em, but you would hear 'em above that fog. That is the things we kind of learned. We learned how to take care. If you had moccasins, you learned how to take care of your moccasins. If they got good and wet then you learned how to rub them back so they were soft again. And you learned how they dried their meat, how they dug their bitterroot and baked their camas and things like that.

We had camas and bitterroot when we was kids, all the time. And right up till after I was married and my mother was still alive, she always had dried meat at home. My dad, lot of times in the summer, would butcher a beef for haying, and then she'd generally dry part of it. And every time my dad or granddad butchered, why my mother and them all dried most of the meat. Sometimes they'd put a lot of it down in kind of a dry salt or something. But they were mostly all dried. So, we had dried meat all the time. I can remember my mother, the flanks, and the bellies of the dried meat, she'd cut it in long strips and dry it. Then lots of time she'd chop that up in chunks and boil it, make a kind of a soup and dumplings with it. I can always remember that. But us kids always run around with a few camas in our pocket and a bitterroot. Jay Swaney said he used to go up to Leon School with a big chunk of dry meat in his hip pocket when he was in the first grade. Things like that. Just Indians lived close to nature.

You could tell an Indian tomorrow he'd be dead, or he'd die in a week from now. It never worried him. He took it as it come. Everything they done pertained to nature. A lot of their habits were learned from animals or birds. Or they'll see a bird doing a certain thing, a duck or something, well that's the way of protecting himself or something. When they wanted to give a boy his medicine, he'd camp and go up in these hills with nothing. He'd camp there. No water and nothing to eat. And he'd sleep there. And when he'd wake up in the morning, there would either be a bird or an animal that would be close to him and singing some kind of medicine song in Indian. When he'd come back to his camp, he always called that his medicine. If it was any kind of bird or animal — a coyote, a wolf or anything like that — why that would be his medicine. And when he would come to a dance, if it was an animal he would generally have a fur on his arm when he danced, and that was the medicine he had. That was done all through, years and years ago. Before I was ever born, they used that quite a bit, I suppose. I remember one time there was an old Kootenai Indian, he'd dance and he always had a red fox on his arm. I don't know — I imagine it was my grandmother one time — she said, "That's his medicine." That's what he had when he come out. They believed in a lot of that kind of stuff.

An old Nez Perce woman stayed with my uncle, and she died. She was supposed to have been a great medicine woman. And the old Indian believed that to this day. They were on a buffalo hunt and they were about to be surrounded by the Blackfeet. She got her medicine working and they got a violent storm, which gave 'em a chance to get away. She done another few things like that. While she was staying with my uncle, a ditch run right in front of the house. And in a thunderstorm she'd be out to that ditch and she would have all the otter skins. She'd keep dipping that in the water, and then she would holler just like them big black woodpeckers with a red top. And she'd holler just like one of them. I think that must have been her medicine.

Just like the blue jay dances, medicine dances, things like that. Like their dances they all pertain to something. They have — some them call it a prayer dance, some call it a jump dance — because they jump just like the black tailed deer. Some call it the back tailed dance. Well they do that in the winter, on New Year's. They all get together and they pray and they have a big feed. At midnight they all shake hands, and shoot their guns or whatever they got. And then the leader starts to sing, and he'll go around and, pretty soon, they'll all get behind him, and this jump dance. And he'll get through, and maybe another fellow will get up there, and maybe he will say a prayer. It's for better livin' and healthier livin' and maybe to get rid of the bad winter.

The bitterroot, they dug that in the spring. The Indian way of that was that they'd send somebody out to see when it was ready to dig. And they went, come back, and told 'em, and they'd have a feast and a prayer. Praying to the bitterroot and for the good health of all the people and all of that. And they'd have this feast after that. And after that, anybody could go out and dig bitterroot, but you wasn't supposed to do that until the feast was done.

And then later on in the year, in the camas prairie country, there was a lot of camas flowers there. Was just a tall plant with a blue flower on the top. Looking at it from a long ways off, a good patch of it you would think it was water. Well then, they'd go and dig camas and they'd take and peel that and they would build a big fire in the ground after it was all washed and taken care of. My Aunt Maggie said, when she was a girl, they'd used these big leaves of the skunk cabbage, they called it. They would lay that on top of the hot rocks and they put the camas on there. Covered with some leaves, and then they'd cover that over with more dirt and leave it there for a couple of days. When they'd take the top off, the camas was cooked. After it was baked it was brown, but it would have a sweet taste.

Of course, the other stuff like choke cherries and that stuff. It was all different ways to cook that up. Choke cherries they'd pound that up. Huckleberries, they'd dried that. No such thing as canning then. And they knew just when to do that, and when the wild strawberries was startin' to ripen, they knew that was when the fawns and elk calves was to be born.

The Salish and Pend d'Oreille kind of thought they was a little bit above the Kootenai. But the deal was, it was their environment and the way they were raised that made the difference, just like they had different habits. You could have a Kootenai come in and visit you for two or three hours, you sit down and have him eat dinner with you. The minute he get through eating, he would put on his hat and go home. And that's where that thing come up, a lot of people would say, "Well, I'm going to be like a Kootenai. I'm going to grab my hat and go home," after he would eat, and that's where that come from. But they were, and the Kootenais in a way were less, kind of a nomadic family. And they were kind of a colonized [communal] family.

There is quite a bit you get to know, especially from the older people. Just like the Kootenai people, I lived around 'em, went with 'em. But they're different. A Kootenai is what you kind of call a nomad. Any place they go is home to 'em. They were great hunters, trappers, and things like that. They didn't care too much about settlin' in one place. And if one had something to eat, they all had something to eat.

I remember, I drove mail stage from Elmo to Nirada with sleighs one winter. And then I'd take a team and go up in the hills, and I'd get a load of logs. When I brought them in, each one got some wood out of that. That would have been a Pend d'Oreille or a Flathead, he would have tried to stick his neighbors for some of that wood — that was the difference. Same way, if they had something to eat, they all had something to eat. If you wanted to hire anybody, them ranchers would want a hay hand, or build a lot of fences, they would just go down to one of them Kootenai camps and say, "I got a bunch two or three miles of fence I'd like built, or a bunch of hay to put up. I'll give you so much to do it." Fine, that's all you would have to say. The next day, he'd be up there with his whole crew. They were all gamblers. Every one of 'em, they like to gamble. They were kind of a happy sort of outfit. I lived with them more than I did with my own people. Course when I was small, I was with a lot of these little Pend d'Oreille kids here.

But then, in 1916, I went over there, and I'd stay right there with the Kootenais. The Kootenais could be down beating one of their neighbors, but somebody go in there and ask him about something, and about that certain person, he'd never know nothing. Someone might say, "Ol' John over here wasn't worth a damn, or some damn thing." Then somebody say, "I want to know something about John." You go to the same guy that made that statement, hell he never knew nothing. I remember one time they come down there looking for a boy stole a horse from a Chinaman up in Canada. Sheriff went down to see where these people was, and they didn't know nothing, course they knew right where that horse was and everything, but it turned out after, the fellers that wanted the horse thought he was a good buy, he was a gentle little pinto. By golly, by the time they got it ready to try to buy him, found out there's international law connected with that, it would cost four or five times the horse's worth to take him to court.

My aunt had the horse, and she told these fellows that wanted him, she said, "All I want is my feed and my twenty dollars." And by golly, when they got to look that over, why it was going to cost 'em lot of money, so they give up. So the little horse stayed right there at the ranch there, and died of old age. Hell, they're awful togetherness, they had their celebrations they tried to be all there. Even their wakes and stuff, they was always there. And well everything they done, they had to do it to exist. They had to do their trapping, course they were natural built for that. A lot of good lumber-jacks amongst them. The only thing that I noticed difference between the Kootenais and ours, when I was working for Bruns he hired ol' Sacalee Finley to put up some rye hay. So he come in with his camp, and next morning he come over to the house. He said, "I got to have some meat," so they run a dry cow in, they butchered her and the next day, there was a wire fence in front of their camp, that meat was all hung on the fence, they sun dried it and our people here dry theirs with fire. And they were quite a study, they were.

The Pend d'Oreilles and Salish were different in this way. See the Pend d'Oreilles was here when the old Hudson's Bay Post started in '47, there was a lot of Pend d'Oreilles here then. So, then the real Salish didn't come in until after Charlo and Arlee moved out of the Bitterroot. You could go down to the church on a church day, and you could pick them guys out. Take them Salish Indians, most of them, they might have a suit of clothes on, or he might have a nice coat, he would always have brand new moccasins on. And a lot of them fellers would have their hat with three quarter tie with a ribbon, a handkerchief on their hat, you could always tell 'em. And you could pick them Salish out, right the minute when they would walk into church. A lot of the Pend d'Oreille and Salish kind of went and helped themselves individually, where the Kootenais stayed kind of colonized [communal]. And a Kootenai, didn't take long for him to move, he could take his outfit and he would be gone in no time, because he didn't have much to move with. And course, I suppose we never noticed our own people, because we were around 'em so much. And then the Nez Perce, he was another fellow that was pretty much that way. A Nez Perce Indian is a hard guy to get acquainted with. I went to school with a lot of them in the boarding school. I went to Chemawa, Oregon, one year, and I went to Tacoma, Washington, two, three years. And there was a lot of 'em Nez Perce in Tacoma. And, by god, they were the hardest Indian kids to get acquainted with. And the kids from the Blackfoot, Browning were the easiest.

There would be church celebrations for Christmas, all the holidays, Easter, Corpus Christi, St. Ignatius day. St. Ignatius day, that's what these fellows are trying to pull up here now. Up until the thirties, yeah, late in the thirties, St. Ignatius day was a big church day. Lot of people would come to them. After the church, they generally had baseball games or horse races. There was a lot of big horse races then. And that'd go on all evening. And lots of times on the Fourth of July celebration, they'd maybe have some horse racing and maybe match 'em [races] and they'd say, "We'll run it on St. Ignatius day." Well they'd have a lot of races then. And, but it was mainly a church day. And up on our old place there, they'd be all kind of camps there going back and forth. The Indians here were all pretty much with the Jesuits. We didn't have any outside, but down on the Nez Perce, and I think on the Spokane, I think there was a lot of Presbyterians. I think it was just which missionaries got into your country first. Like southern Idaho, I think southern Idaho got in with a lot of Mormons there, to start with.

Before the homesteaders came in 1910, some of the old Indians had little gardens, and well they, some of them I guess went more to preserving, drying their fruit, and stuff like that. But, I think quite a few of them older ones they had gardens, of course they didn't live like they do now in bunches. Each Indian lived on his own place. He lived up along these creeks. In the winter time, lots of times we'd wonder where they were. One time said to my mother, "I wonder where old so and so is." She said, "He's in the timber." So, the one's that had their place out on the creek, they'd move into the timber, because they were closer to wood and were in the shelter from the wind and everything. They'd stay there until spring broke, and then go back down there on their places.

Some of them up there around Dayton, and Elmo, up there in Somers in the early days, those Kootenai there. They lived along the lake, some of them moved away from the lake, and lived up along them creeks, like Dayton Creek. There was five or six or eight or maybe more families up Dayton Creek. And Valley Creek, there was a lot of Indians up in there, up Crow Creek, there was a lot of Indians along Crow Creek. Hammers and Red Horns and Beaverheads, and Chief Eagles, and some Finleys, different ones in there. But these, this bunching up in this housing deal, I don't know, through health deal, or what it is, they claim they had to centralize for water systems and stuff. But I think they would have been better off, let them go out on little places and build them up. Get 'em away from those housing areas. These housing area, as near as I can see there's no future to them. There's no place for a garden behind 'em. The houses are right next to one another, and there's some of the boys is realizing it, and they're moved away from them. And the ones that stay there, if you ain't got a job, you ain't got nothing, outside of maybe getting these commodities, or something. I didn't like to see it when the housing come in. I thought, if they built a house, build it up some place where you could grow a garden. Pablo had a good start. My grandson started up there and he had a good house, and he had a good big yard with it. He had a lawn, and a little garden spot. But these down here, and them up at Arlee, there just pert' near back to back. And there was a lot, some of the people that would like to get on their own place.

Even before allotment, each Indian lived on their own place. I think it was quite a bit of the teaching of the Jesuits. See they come in to Stevensville and then they branched out and then they went down and that country around Priest River or someplace down there. That's where they wanted to set up a mission, and then they decided they could have had flood damage and things. That's when they changed and moved up here. They established this one in 1854. And they had a lot of Indians following then.

A lot of the Indians got allotments where they were living at. Like where I was born, that's an allotment Joe's dad got. And we had, one, two, there were three allotments there, my three brothers. And up on the foothills where Walter, above Walter's, me and my two sisters was allotted up there. And then from the old Hudson's Bay house down to the creek there, where Webber lives, where my uncle's allotments was there, his wife and two daughters and a son and himself. That's where they were allotted. Over across there where Bearhead

was, that was, that was some of the Dandy Jim family, they were allotted there. So, they, most of them, got a lot of their land where they
were living. My mother and my brother, they were allotted down on
the river, down there by Moiese. But the things changed, everything
changed, farming's changed. Oh, I know one time you could stand
out there by my granddad's, and you could spot four thrashing machines out in the valley. They were thrashing grain. It wasn't made
into hay then. And that's one thing, I think what made so many
water fowls and upland birds, they were.

Well automobiles got in here and the country got fenced up.
White people come in and rented lot of the Indian land. Lot of them
could travel in old Model Ts better than they could horses, and they
just started getting rid of them. And then fox farms and things like
that come in and buy 'em. Depression was on, buy a horse for five
dollars, and they were just selling them everywhere. So that's what
happened to a lot of that.

The traders that I remember was Beckwith and Louie DeMers'
dad, ol' Alex DeMers, and [Addison] Sterling at Ronan, and they
all used to have them big signs above their doors, I think it was "Li-
censed Indian Trader" on 'em. I think on some of these old pictures,
if you get ahold of one, I think you can still see that. I think a feller
by the name of [Fred E.] Peeso, they had a store over at Camas,
and then old [James A.] McGowan was at Plains. Ol' McGowan
was where ol' Michel from Camas Prairie [traded]. My dad said one
time, that he didn't know if ol' Michel knew how many cattle he had
over there. They would sell three year old, four year old steers, and
go down to Plains and get his money from McGowan. And this one
time he was in Plains and his wife and daughter heard dogs barking
and raising heck, and they wouldn't go out there. When he come
home and they told him about it, he went out in this little cabin. And
these fellows found his cash, and they figured it was between 60 and
80 thousand dollars that was taken out of there. They never did find
out who done it. But I suppose some guy was watching him when he
left McGowan's, knew about where his cash was.

The traders got along good with the Indians, and Beckwith
had a deal here on Christmas, that there would be all kinds of raffles
there. And that'd go on all Christmas Eve until midnight mass. God,
harness, saddle, buckskin shirts and gloves, and everything. Some

the store raffled off, some of the individuals would come in and put up their stuff and sell. The crowd would be just bank full there, until midnight mass, and then everything closed up. That was quite a thing.

The traders gave credit to the Indians who got their patents to their place. Then they soaked them to them guys. Three-fourths of them could never redeem them. That's how the stores got 'em. I forgot how many they said Scearce had a one time, quite a bunch of them. Beckwith had a lot of them. Well you have eighty acres out here, and you'd go to one of the moneyed guys, and you say, "I'd like to borrow twenty-five hundred dollars on my eighty," and he would make up a mortgage. Nine times out of ten, you wouldn't be able to pay it off. Then they forced that forced patent on a lot of 'em.

Celebrations

Well up there at Arlee about 1905, they had a parade ever so often during their celebration. I imagine there was over 100 head of horses in that parade of Indians with their outfits on. I can remember that. That old fellow that was standing with them, we stayed at his place. His name was Big Hawk. You see these old camps. They call 'em powwows now. I never liked the name of that. And I never like the name of the tepee. All I can remember, when I was a kid they were all called lodges. The Fourth of July was a get together, it was no powwow. Everybody would go, and a lot of people would come from other reservations. And they'd say, "Well, I'm going up to this celebration and I'm going to stay with old so and so." Well, he didn't even know he was comin'. But he would be just as welcome as could be, and they'd make room for him. And that's why they done it. It was kind of a get together. It was a lot of people, maybe from some other reservation, hadn't been here for five or six years. It's kind of a reunion is was what it was. They'd come there. Take in the celebration. Some of them would dance there. And maybe they'd just set there and visit.

People wore fancy beaded outfits to the celebrations. I did take Eneas Conko and old Sam Tilden, and I believe it was Eneas Grandjo. I took them to Hot Springs for the *Life* magazine wanted pictures of the bathhouse, that was right after it was built. Old Sam had an awful beautiful beaded outfit that he danced with. So, when I went to get him why he had this buckskin outfit on, that's in this picture. So, I said, "Sam, I thought you were going to wear that nice beaded outfit." "No," he said, "that's to dance with," but he said, when you went to anything important, he said you always wore one of these outfits. But unfortunately, the darn pictures was all taken and then they were taking the films into Missoula and they lost 'em all. So, I had to go back there and then the next month I think it was, and I just took two of them. I didn't take Sam back.

Because I remember an old Nez Perce and his wife, come up from Lapwai, Idaho for the celebration. They were going to stay with this old fellow [Paul] Charlo. Paul's wife had passed away in the meantime, and he was living alone. So, this old feller come up and his wife was kind of plain. He said, "We come up to stay with Paul." They come up on the bus. He said, "Paul told us we could stay in his lodge over there, and we went over there and there was nothing there, you couldn't cook there or nothing. I had to hire a feller to take us to town so we could get something to eat." So, I visited with him a little while, and I said, "Why don't you come home with me tonight?" So, he did, him and his wife, they come back here and stayed all night, and then I took 'em to the agency and he said he always figured he had some land up on Crow Creek. And he give the Indian name, but they could never locate it. He said he was full blood Nez Perce, but he never left the Bitterroot, until he was eighteen years old, I think.

Anyhow, when Joseph was coming over the trail on his retreat, this old [Albert Thomas] Moore told me that his mother begged Joseph to turn around and go back, but he wouldn't do it. He said he was going to Canada. Canada that the queen mother would take care of them. So, he just kept traveling. Joseph was in about forty miles of where he wanted to go. If he would have made that other forty miles, he would have been alright. Then I took Moore over to the depot, and he went on home. He was one of the old fellers, figured Paul had everything there, cooking and everything. But he didn't. It was quite a bit like that. And then you would see so many tribes. I could see the Shoshoni, the Bannacks, the Crees, the Salish, the Kootenai, the Nez Perce, the Umatillas. They'd be people there from all different tribes.

There were a lot of differences in celebrations back then. You didn't have no card games. That was out. And the chief was the head guy. He'd get up in the morning, and he'd either do it himself or he'd have somebody. He'd get on a horse and he'd ride all around the camp and he'd tell 'em what was going to happen that day, whether they were going to dance or what they were going to do. And then at night, there'd be a bunch of them (maybe 20 or 30 head of horses in a bunch). They'd all be in a bunch group, singing and go around the camp. Maybe a man would have some woman on riding behind him.

Then when that was over, of course they didn't have any electric lights then. So, when that was over, they would beat the canvas, they called it. Indians had a name for it. They'd sing from each lodge to the other, and they would do that all night. And then in the morning just as they got through, why they would wake everybody up. And then if you lost anything, why the guy would come around horseback. He might have it with him or he might tell you where it was. You'd go over to the chief's lodge or where it was and claim whatever you had. And nobody lost anything then. It was all done.

When we had the St. Ignatius Mission centennial up home [1954], we had four for five of them old people there that had their camps there. There was a woman then from Alberta up there in Canada, and she was all excited. She said had come and watched the Indian dance and she took pictures, and they left. And I think they got pret' near to Missoula before she discovered she lost her handbag. She said all her credentials was in it, money, and everything. She was pretty excited. So, she come back. I said, "Where was you at." She said, "It was kind of a little higher ridge on one side than where the camps were." We had about pretty close to a hundred lodges there, out on our old meadow. She said, "Out over along that hill." Well that was right where all these old people was camped. So, a feller by the name of Frank Combs was there. He talked good Indian. I said, "Frank, go with them over there. See if any of them seen it." So, he went to two or three camps. No, they never seen anything. This old lady [Sophie] Moiese, she lived in Arlee, close to the old Jocko Agency. And she was quite a noted old lady. Everybody liked her. A lot of the university people would come out and visit her. She couldn't talk much English, but they could understand what she had. So, they finally went to her lodge and asked her if she found anything like it. "Yeah," she described it. She said, "I got it in there in my trunk." So, they went and got it for her. I told 'em, "Well, I knew, if it was an old person got it, you'd be sure to get it back." I wouldn't have said anything about, if it had been a young guy you might not have gotten it. But, that's the way they were. And on Sunday there was nothing in the morning. Used to have a big tent camp east of here. One morning I said to my mother, "I wonder where everybody is." She said, "Oh, they're in church." And that was one thing, on Sunday morning you all had to go to church. That was a must. There was nothing done until afternoon.

And then if anybody happened to pass away, everything stopped right then. And that's the way the old timers done it. There was no such thing as card game. They'd have horse races, foot races in the evening, something like that. Then they would do their different dances. Of course, they all had nice outfits. You don't see them anymore, just a few of them. Most of my Indian stuff was just learned about what they done and how they lived and things like that.

That's why I say that to be a good school teacher, where you got a lot of Indian children. You pret' near got to know 'em, you got to pret' near know Indian. An Indian child, if you encourage him to come and get in with you, he will. But if you don't, he'll stand back, and that's why there is a lot of dropouts of kids. They just won't mix, and the kids don't have time to try to get him in. Unless he is an exceptional athlete of some kind, well then they will get him. That's one thing. And they got to mix. They got to mix. This idea of segregating 'em, it won't work. It never has and won't. Because I went to these government schools. You had Indians from all over the United States and up in Alaska. And they were never segregated then. Boy, they'd have quite a time and after a while they'd get so they could talk to one another. I know the first time out in Chemawa, Oregon, I had two boys from above Nome, Alaska. Heck, one of them wasn't there a month, and he knew all the slang in the school. That's the way they are.

No, it wasn't segregated then. But then, they brought a bunch of Navajos up there and they tried that on them. They brought an interpreter with them, and they took 'em clear away from the other Indian kids. But it didn't work out. I know when I went to school in Ronan along about 1908 or 1909, old Charlie Michel, he was kind of a chief of the Pend d'Oreille, his boy went to school up there, Louie. He had long braids and his dad didn't want 'em to cut his hair. And he couldn't talk English, and I and a feller by the name of

Louie Vallee, we'd interpret for him. And I don't think it was no time at all, there was a feller runn' the store. I worked for Scearce's store. He had two boys about his age and they all got to pallin' together. They were white boys, and I believe every corner of the old building around there you could see where old Louie Michel wrote his name. And just being with those kids.

Chapter 8
Life as an Elder

In this country [St. Ignatius], it's all new now. You go out here and very few people that was here. And the old Indians is all passed away and gone, and there is just a few of them left. So that's why they are trying to get this culture deal started now. To get a lot the hymns back that they used at the wakes and what the wakes and everything meant to the people and things like that. And then they're trying to bring back a lot of their old dances and all of their old meaning. And Clarence Woodcock up here in the center has got a book made up of all different plants and what they're used for. I think he's got the Latin name and the Indian name to 'em. And he had a slide up there last winter, and they had it all on the slide, color pictures, and then they narrated as they went along. And that's quite a deal.

I was telling you how it used to be that when anybody passed away, then the old timers would announce it at the funeral that there would be a feast and whoever's home it was to be. So then you all went there and they generally had a big circle there. And if it was bad weather, they'd have two, three lodges put together, make one kind of a big shelter. It wasn't like now. They'd have a big circle outside, then the women would pass the grub to each family, and then they would have their prayers first of course. Then the old chief or some of these MCs would do the speaking. And after the dinner, why then they'd bring out the deceased's belongings. Then they would give maybe a hat or a shirt or horse, or something to different one of the friends. And that's the way that went.

And my uncle Duncan's boy [Peter Colville McDonald] died in 1905. We were all up to the celebration at Arlee, and we were living in the camp with Big Hawks, Jerome Big Hawk and his dad.

Charlie's uncle, Duncan McDonald and Duncan's son, Peter.

Source: Toole Archives, Mansfield Library,
University of Montana, Missoula,
photograph MS 562, 13-3

Charlie's uncle, Duncan McDonald.

Source: Montana Historical Society Photograph Archives, Helena, Montana,
photograph 943-624

Duncan's lodge was right next to ours. Peter was fairly ill then, so they had the side of the lodge flaps up, so that it was cool in the lodge. Ever once in a while, he'd ask me to go down to the nice big clear ditch then, that's where we got our water. So, we would go and get the water for him, and he could lay there and watch 'em out there, what was going on. So then not long after we got home, I believe it was in August some time, he passed away. My uncle was living down there where Max Johnson is now. So, they announced a feast and that was real late. I think it was a month or so afterwards. And they had all, they prepared that thing for pret' near a week. It was a big one. And I was up with my folks, when I was a kid up here to Crow Creek to two or three different feasts there. The big thing for us kids was when my mom or them would come back, we'd have to get into the sacks she'd bring home, because we'd have dried meat in there, maybe fried bread, and I was always looking for the dried meat. And maybe a little bunch of camas or different things. So that was the way the feasts was run, as I remember 'em. And at that time, everything was given out to the deceased's personal friends. But now it's changed, they have a funeral and then they have a giveaway right after the dinner. Well, we never had that before. Of course, in the early days, there was a lot of nice fancy outfits, beaded outfits, buckskin outfits, lot of eagle feathers, and things like that.

The younger Indians don't bake the camas like the old ones. They used to have a lot of that. We had it all the time at home, us kids have two or three bulbs of that in our pockets all the time. We always had bitterroot, and, of course, when I was a kid, all our huckleberries was dried, there was no such things as jars. There was a lot of fruit like that, but it changed. Camas, baked camas, and bitterroot and stuff like that, you very seldom see it anymore. Culture is trying to bring it back. Camas Prairie was where they got all their camas. There was a strip down there when the weather was real — good wet year — and you'd look out in there, and you'd swear it was a kind of a little reservoir, because you could see that blue on there, and it would be all bloom from the camas.

It's just like tanning hides, nobody wants to tan a hide anymore. The only place you can buy tanned deer hides is up at Elmo. All our people down here, they won't fool with it. It's too much work. An Indian now, instead of drying his meat, he'll take a runner up to one of them guys, and he'll cut it up for him, and he'll put it in his freezer. So, you don't find too much dried meat, once in a while somebody will dry some, but not too often. The only people who stayed kind of by their old ways is the Kootenais. But that was their life, what the Kootenais didn't have the things we had down here. That's why there's so many trappers amongst them, hunters, and all woods workers, and things like that. We'd get apples once in a while from the Fathers here, but then my dad planted a few fruit trees, and some berry bushes. But most everything we had was wild.

In that Horseshoe Bend country there is an area called the Nez Perce home site where Allicott had his cabin. There was an old dugout canoe set there for years. Joe Gardipe was having some arts and craft deal in that Indian Dance every year, west of Polson, so I wanted him to get it. I said you go get it, take it up to your place, it would make a nice flower bed. The back end of it was kind of rotted out. So, I told [Forrest] Stone about it, let's see, no, it wasn't Stone either, I guess it was [C. C.] Wright. Anyhow it was one of the superintendents. I told him about it. He got all excited. He said, "I'm going to send a road crew up there." They went up there, and they crated it. They brought it down here to the church, and they set it alongside of the fence there, during the centennial in '54. And then they sent it to Helena to the historical outfit. Then some young fellers over there said that they were going to rebuild it with wood filler so that it'd look like it did in the first place. But I went back there a year or two after, and they hadn't done anything to it. It was setting down in the basement. And that dugout canoe, my brother John and my dad, he told me. I heard him mention a couple of times about, they would go down to the river and one of them Nez Perce would come across in a dugout canoe, and they would swim their horses across, and he'd take them across in a canoe. These old canoes was dug out of a log, out of a big cottonwood log. This one up there at Allicott still had a lot of the old axe marks on it. So, I don't know if they ever done anymore with it or not.

Allicott was there until about 1910 or 1911. Jackson Sundown had a place right close there, and an old Kiyula he settled down there on Crow Creek, right there where they call it Rocky Butte now. He had that place right across there, that was an old campground. And old Kiyula was an uncle to Pat Adams' mother, and he lived there

Charles Duncan McDonald, as an elder.

Source:
Sélis Qlispé Culture Committee, St. Ignatius, Montana

Charles Duncan McDonald.

Source:
Maggie Goode, Lonepine, Montana.

until he died, and he's buried up here. I think Jackson stayed around Umatilla part of the time, but I think he was down on the Snake River, or someplace when he died.

I got this picture of old Sam Tilden and Jackson Sundown. I understand they was hid under a buffalo robe when they had the fight in the Big Hole. And Sam's family, when they surrendered over in the Bear Paws, why they got away. They went up into Fort Mc-Leod, and they stayed there, for, I think he said, a couple of years. Duncan, my dad's older brother was living at Ravalli then, he went up and got 'em. They come down to Ravalli and stayed with Duncan a year or two, then they went back to Lapwai, Idaho.

When we had this centennial at Post Creek in '47, Sam had that outfit on. After he got back, he sent Mrs. Wipru a picture of when he was young, so she put the young face in that outfit. And when he found that we was related to him, I come home one day and she give us that for a Christmas present. It had a thousand dollar tag for the university, when we got it. And when we had the centennial, she had a lot of paintings, big ones like that, mostly of the southwest and Browning. We had a museum in the old house. By golly, she left us a lot of paintings, and a quite a few little Navaho rugs. When everything was over, we couldn't find her. So, we finally located her at Swan Lake. We got her stuff all back to her. Then never heard from her for a long time. One day she walked over to the house, and she'd said she'd been in the southwest and wasn't feeling good. So, she thought she'd start a studio in Missoula. So, she got in Missoula, and she said, she just couldn't stand it. So, they moved out on the Jocko River, up in the canyon. She said, "I just fell for that place, and I felt good there." That's where she had her studio when she died.

I was never down in the Idaho countries, or where the [Nez Perce] reservation was till five or six years ago. Pete Tenas' wife died, and a lot of cousins from Nirada was going down to the funeral, to him and his family. And he stopped to get me. She was to be buried at Kamiah, Idaho. And that was my first time down there. So, after the funeral, I got to talking to two or three women. I said, "Well, I've been over eighty years getting this far, and I never got down here before." Well, what part of it I seen was pretty rough, hilly country. But after you get down to Lewiston, that's where we turned off, we didn't go into Lewiston. We went up to Moscow and out that way.

But looking at it from the top of one of them divides, kind of looked like south of Lewiston, look like some pretty nice country. Looked like some nice farms out there.

And just like somebody said here a few years back, Reagan made the statement. What they give to the Indians. They never give any land to the Indians, the Indians owned that before they come. And they took it away from us, like they took the Bitterroot Valley. The Nez Perce, they took the northeast corner of Oregon, the Snake River, they took that away from Chief Joseph's father. They done that in the Black Hills with the Sioux. Over here the Sweet Grass, Charlie Gerard showed me a book the other day, and the old chief that was with that part of them that told how he relinquished all the Sweet Grass holdings to the government, because they were to take care of his tribe with provisions. And that was right about the time that there was quite a starvation among the Blackfeet people. And then over on the west side of the Blackfeet was, when the miners had a big pull with the Senator. Guess that's when they got in on that part of Glacier Park, because they figured it was a big mining deal. Which it fell through, and then become a park. And but that's the way everything set as I remember.

Editors' Note

On January 2, 1995, Charlie died of natural causes at the St. Luke Community Hospital in Ronan. He was buried in the St. Ignatius Catholic Cemetery. His body was later moved to the cemetery in Lonepine where his eldest daughter, Charlotte, had been buried in 1938.

Further Readings and Sources

Some sources about McDonald family history and Flathead Reservation history in the twentieth century can provide further information for interested readers.

The life of Charlie's McDonald grandfather and a collection of his grandfather's writings has been published in Steve A. Anderson, *Angus McDonald of the Great Divide: The Uncommon Life of a Fur Trader, 1816-1889* (Coeur d'Alene, Idaho: Museum of North Idaho Press, 2011).

A biography of Duncan McDonald, Charlie's uncle, is Robert Bigart and Joseph McDonald, *Duncan McDonald: Flathead Indian Reservation Leader and Cultural Broker, 1849-1937* (Pablo, Montana: Salish Kootenai College Press, 2016).

An autobiographical narrative by Charlie's aunt was published in Christina MacDonald McKenzie Williams, "The Daughter of Angus MacDonald," *Washington Historical Quarterly*, vol. 13, no. 2 (April 1922), pages 107-117.

Charlie made several references to his Aunt Maggie telling him about the great trout fishing at the Flathead Lake dam site at the foot of the lake. Alex. Staveley Hill described some fishing trips by Mrs. Baptiste Eneas and Mrs. Angus McDonald and their families in 1883, and their fishing success at the dam site. See Alex. Staveley Hill, *From Home to Home: Autumn Wanderings in the North-West, in the Years 1881, 1882, 1883, 1884* (New York: O. Judd Co., 1885), pages 367-380.

Short family histories of Charlie's maternal grandfather and maternal great-grandfather can be found in Robert J. Bigart, editor, *Life and Death at St. Mary's Mission, Montana: Births, Marriages,*

Deaths, and Survival among the Bitterroot Salish Indians, 1866-1891 (Pablo, Montana: Salish Kootenai College Press, 2005), pages 259-260 (Deschamps), and 321-322 (Rodgers).

Charlie's father-in-law, Charles William Berry, was Missoula County Sheriff in the 1880s. See Robert Raffety and John C. Moe, *Sheriffs of Missoula County, Montana, and Their Times, 1860 to 1978* (Missoula, Montana: n.p., 1988?), pages 96-101.

Charlie's mother-in-law stayed with Sophie Morigeau, a mixed blood trader in the Tobacco Plains country in northwest Montana. See Rebecca Timmons, et. al., "The History and Archaeology of Sophie Morigeau," *Archaeology in Montana*, vol. 42, no. 1 (2001), pages 1-53.

Charlie talked about the early twentieth century roundup of the Pablo buffalo herd for shipment to Canada. The open range was ending with the opening of the reservation to white homesteaders in 1910. There are many sources about the roundup, but he refers specifically to Thomas W. Jones, *The Last of the Buffalo: Comprising a History of the Buffalo Herd of the Flathead Reservation and an Account of the Last Great Buffalo Roundup* (Cincinnati, Ohio: Tom Jones, 1909, reprinted 2001, Doug Allard's Flathead Indian Museum & Trading Post, St. Ignatius, Montana).

The killing of four Indian hunters and a game warden in the Swan Valley in 1908 is covered in Selis Qlispe Culture Committee, "The Swan Massacre: A Brief History," in Upper Swan Valley Historical Society, Inc., *The Gathering Place: Swan Valley's Gordon Ranch* (Condon, Montana: Upper Swan Valley Historical Society, 2017), pages 62-93.

A survey of reservation history in the first half of the twentieth century with quotes from many tribal elders was published in Thompson Smith, "A Brief History of Kerr Dam and the Reservation," in David Rockwell, ed., *clqétk ntx étks a kinmituk: The Lower Flathead River, Flathead Indian Reservation, Montana: A Cultural, Historical, and Scientific Resource* (Pablo, Mont.: Salish Kootenai College Tribal History Project, 2008), pages 18-37. The background for the early years of the administration of the Flathead Irrigation Project and the political battle over the leasing of the Flathead Lake dam site is given in Garrit Voggesser, *Irrigation, Timber, and Hydropower: Negotiating Natural Resource Development on the Flathead Indian*

Reservation, Montana, 1904-1945 (Pablo, Montana: Salish Kootenai College Press, 2017).

For the history of the Ninemile Remount station of the United States Forest Service see Jane Reed Benson, *Thirty-two Years in the Mule Business: The USDA/Forest Service Remount Depot and Winter Range* (Missoula, Montana: U.S. Forest Service, Northern Region, 1980).

The 1916 citizenship ceremony at Dixon that Charlie talked about, was covered in "Indians Made American Voters," *The Daily Missoulian*, June 11, 1916, p. 1, c. 1; p. 3, c. 1-2.

The life story of Albert Thomas Moore, the Nez Perce elder who came to the Arlee powwow to visit Paul Charlo, was told in Anthony E. Thomas, *Pi-Lu'-Ye-Kin: The Life History of a Nez Perce Indian*, Anthropological Studies No. 3 (Washington, D.C.: American Anthropological Association, 1970).

Two obituaries for Charlie are "Charles D. McDonald," *Missoulian*, January 3, 1995, page B3; and "Tribal Elder Charlie Mc-Donald Left Behind History, Memories," *Char-Koosta News* (Pablo, Montana), January 20, 1995, page 1, col. 2-6; page 3, col. 1-4.

Index

T

tanning hides 120
Tenas, Pete 124
Thompson 68
Thompson Falls Dam 87
Tilden, Sam 22, 112–113, 124
timber 67
traders 111–112
trapping 85
treaties 81, 125
tribal council 65–67, 69–70, 72–73
Tunison, George, tribal lawyer 48

U

Ursuline nuns 31
U.S. Bureau of Indian Affairs 64, 73
U.S. Forest Service 51–64

V

Vallee 70
Vallee, Louie 116
Vanderburg, Jerome 104

W

Waylan boys 91
welfare 74–75
Wheeler Howard Act 42, 65, 67, 70, 72, 80
Whispering Charlie, Mary 48
Whiting, Ruth 84
Wipru, Mrs. 124
Woodcock, Clarence 117
World War I 36
World War II 39
Wright, C. C., superintendent 121

Y

Yellow Mountain 47–49